THE END
OF AN ERA

REDISCOVERING A HIDDEN HISTORY

Dr. Ana Méndez Ferrell

Voice of The Light Ministries

DEDICATION

I dedicate this book to my dear Heavenly Father, to whom I owe all things, and to Jesus Christ, my savior who brought me out of darkness and revealed His light to me. I will always be thankful for giving me His Spirit, his wisdom, health, and all the riches of His glory to share His love and power with others.

Voice of The Light Ministries

Category	Eschatology
Publisher	Voice of The Light Ministries P.O. Box 3418 Ponte Vedra, Florida, 32004 United States of America
	www.VoiceOfTheLight.com

ISBN 978-1-933163-82-6

CONTENTS

COMMENTS

Today, a new generation is emerging demanding truth, pushing us to seek the power and the establishment of The Kingdom of God in a much deeper way. That is why The Father is raising up a generation that understands His eternal purpose. A generation that is willing to establish their lives upon the foundations which Jesus Christ, as Apostle and Administrator of all things, left us and entrusted us with: THE CHURCH.

"THE END OF AN ERA" is a very serious study and investigation carried out by Dr. Ana Méndez Ferrell. It sheds light upon and brings together an infinite number of biblical truths that have been perverted by religiosity and the ignorance of many regarding the end times. You will witness how even history backs up every one of the words Jesus Christ announced through His prophets as well as those He spoke with while here on earth.

No doubt you hold in your hands an invaluable complement that will help you unearth in your spirit each one of the eternal principles Jesus established for a Governing Church; finishing all things in His death and resurrection.

As young people and being part of this generation of Reformers, we are called to shake off all structures and preconceived ideas so that the Spirit of God can introduce to our understanding, and that of our nations, a new Genesis.

It's Time for Reformation!

David Silva Rios, Guayaquil-Ecuador

Every prophet in the old covenant understood history in detail, either through culture or revelation. Their prophecies never belittled the understanding of what God "did," so that through revelation what He would "do" could be understood. As the church, we have lost that historical account, that thread, and without it, it is impossible to understand the purpose of His multi-generational plan we were inserted into.

The book you hold in your hands is a decisive text whose pages manifest the sincere dedication to inquire truth. With deep love, Prophet Ana Méndez Ferrell joins two realms, the historical as well as revelation in an apostolic way while shedding light on the historical and spiritual construction of the building called church. We will not see this in its fullness until we understand what has already been fulfilled.

I venture to say that after reading each chapter, you will not see the crucifixion, resurrection or the true prophecies about Jesus in the same way. A powerful gust of understanding will elevate your faith to experience the supernatural Kingdom that Christ completely conquered.

Simón Aquino M., Santiago - Chile

INTRODUCTION

This is probably one of the most important books you have ever had in your hands.

The search for truth as well as understanding the origin of what we believe is fundamental in order to walk with God.

We are living in times that demand serious investigations and radical changes. The Church and its members - I'm speaking in general terms-are not epistles of the glory of God that the world can read. Far from it, the world is not seeing much difference between those who call themselves Christians and the rest of the people.

You find the sick in both groups, along with people with the same kinds of problems with no apparent solution. You also find the same people full of debt, living in lack and the same types of sin and abominations that are seen in and out of Church. The Church is fragmented and attacks itself from within. The essence of what could be is not seen.

Shortly after receiving the glorious Gospel of Jesus Christ, the Church of Galatia in the Bible were "enchanted," "bewitched" by religious defilers that caused them to return to the law and conform to a system that leads them to the death of the spirit.

I marvel that you are turning away so soon from Him who called you in the grace of Christ, to a different gospel, which is not another; but there are some who trouble you and want to pervert the gospel of Christ.

But even if we, or an angel from heaven, preach any other gospel to you than what we have preached to you, let him be accursed.

Galatians 1: 6-8

If this happened in the first century in just a few years among the most glorious Church there has ever been, can you imagine the type of distortion that has happened after two thousand years?

The Church lost the basic principles of interpretation when the dependence on the Holy Spirit was lost. That is why we have been dragging around many erroneous fables and doctrines that have robbed the effectiveness of the finished work of Christ.

As I sought answers to deep questions that arose in my spirit, God led me to rediscover history.

We must see and analyze the things that really occurred and were actually written as a testimony of the fulfillment of all the prophecies regarding the end of the Old Testament age.

These facts have always been accessible to us, and others before me have attempted to bring them to the light, but the devil, as well as dogmas and time have kept them from being made known.

This book is an extract and a historical summary that will open your eyes to see and understand that many things which the Church is still waiting for to take place, have already occurred. Christ was clear when He said:

I have glorified You on the earth. I have finished the work which You have given Me to do.

John 17:4

He finished His work and does not have to do anything else to finish it!

Reading the works of the historian, *Flavius Josephus* is a great and heavy task since they are written in old English with a grammatical form that is no longer used. They are written in 27 books and have been translated several times by different people, which mean not all versions are exactly the same.

The essence and content is the same, but the grammatical form may vary.

For this reason, and knowing that very few people have delved into such deep investigations, I decided to extract the more relevant chapters and paragraphs which certify what took place in the first century.

In some cases I was forced to translate from Old English to Modern English, while making sure I did not touch the meaning of each phrase.

The origin and page numbers of each extract are clearly identified in the notes on the pages so that the reader may clearly verify:

The version I will be referring to is:

The War of the Jews:
The History of the Destruction of Jerusalem
by Flavius Josephus.

As I read many versions, I found the content to be the same in all of them but not the order of the books. One may find an episode at the end of a chapter that in other versions is in the beginning of the next chapter and even in the next book.

So I encourage you, if you want to go beyond and deeper in this truth, to read on your own the complete works of Flavius Josephus.

May the eyes of your understanding be opened and may you enter into the wholeness, which was conquered by Christ on the cross and the glories which followed His sufferings.

THE END OF AN ERA

Much has been speculated regarding the end times, as if referring to the end of the world. The truth is, when Jesus spoke of this topic, He was referring to the end of an era.

Who was Jesus and what did He come to do on earth?

This question, which seems very obvious in Christian circles, is not understood as it should be. In fact, there is much confusion as far as His purpose and design.

Jesus was the prophesied Messiah of Israel and His ministry in the flesh was only for the Jews.

In the spirit, as King of Kings, He is the Messiah of all humanity, but in the flesh, He was circumscribed to the people of Israel.

> *But He answered and said, "I was not sent except to the lost sheep of the house of Israel."*
>
> *Matthew 16:24*

Jesus, which is the Spirit of Prophecy, prophesied about Himself throughout the Old Testament. He prophesied about what His coming in the flesh would be like, and how He would defeat sin and establish The Kingdom of God on the earth. Then He would sit as King in high places and bring judgment. This would bring an end to the Old Testament age and would make His tabernacle amongst those who believed in Him, placing His Spirit within them. Everyone who believed in Him would have eternal life.

> *Of this salvation the prophets have inquired and searched carefully, who prophesied of the grace that would come to you, searching what, or what manner of time, **the Spirit of Christ who was in them** was indicating when He testified beforehand the sufferings of Christ and the glories that would follow.*
>
> *1 Peter 1:10-11*

We must find every single interpretation of the words of Jesus spoken in the gospels in the Old Testament, since it was the Spirit of Christ which spoke about them before His coming in the flesh. He came to fulfill EVERYTHING THAT WAS WRITTEN ABOUT HIM and would complete His work.

That is why He said, "It is finished!"

The Purpose Of The Old Testament

This was established by God to prefigure true and celestial things which are The Kingdom of God in the Spirit. God created for Himself a people and a nation. He established prophets which would announce the coming of what was true and immutable, which was the Messiah. Once Jesus Christ came, there was no longer a need for the former things.

For if that first covenant had been faultless, then no place would have been sought for a second.

In that He says, "A new covenant," He has made the first obsolete. Now what is becoming obsolete and growing old is ready to vanish away.

Hebrews 8:7 & 13

For the law, having a shadow of the good things to come, and not the very image of the things, can never with these same sacrifices, which they offer continually year by year, make those who approach perfect.

Hebrews 10:1

Jesus had to come in the flesh to fulfill all justice, be the perfect sacrifice, and to present Himself once and for all. When "Justice" was fulfilled, the purpose of the Old Covenant culminated and Jesus established the new one. Jesus came to establish Himself as the High Priest of the coming age, or the good things to come. Referring to them as "the good things to come," means that the old would end in order to establish the new.

*But Christ came as **High Priest of the good things to come**, with the greater and more perfect tabernacle not made with hands, that is, not of this creation. Not with the blood of goats and calves, but with His own blood He entered the Most Holy Place once for all, having obtained eternal redemption.*

Hebrews 9:11-12

The fulfillment of the work of the cross marked the end of the old system of sacrifice and this was considered the end of the age.

> *He then would have had to suffer often since the foundation of the world;* **but now, once at the end of the ages,** *He has appeared to put away sin by the sacrifice of Himself.*
>
> Hebrews 9:26

Notice that the end of the age is linked to the Cross, and not to the end of the world.

The end of the age had come. The priesthood in the flesh gave way to the Spirit. **Jesus cannot be and could not have been the High Priest in the flesh in the earth because he did not have the priestly lineage the old covenant required.**

> *For every high priest is appointed to offer both gifts and sacrifices. Therefore it is necessary that this One also have something to offer.*
>
> *For if* **He were on earth,** *He would not be a priest, since there are priests who offer the gifts according to the law; who serve the copy and shadow of the heavenly things,*
>
> Hebrews 8:3-5a

This clearly states that the earthly ended so the heavenly could be established.

The physical Temple ended to give way for the Temple of the Spirit to be established in the hearts of men.

Jesus spoke to His contemporaries, especially to His disciples of when the end of the Age would be. Jesus knew that an unprecedented tribulation upon the Jews was coming, which would end the nation of Israel. The Father had determined this would happen in 70 A.D. and the clock was ticking.

Jesus predicted everything that was going to happen. He said, it would be "soon," and it happened 37 years later. All that was fulfilled was described in detail by Flavius Josephus, and that is the reason for this book. The reader should be made aware that everything Jesus spoke of was fulfilled and that everything prophesied regarding the end in the Old Testament was also fulfilled.

Through the first twenty verses in Matthew 24, Jesus tells His disciples about the many events that would accompany His "coming," which relates to the time when the temple was destroyed. Several signs are mentioned. In the parallel verses in Luke 21 and Mark 13, we find also expressions that have been previously prophesied in the Old Testament.

Jesus declared that "The abomination of desolation," first prophesied by Daniel[1], was one of the events that would take place during the times of famine, earthquakes, wars, false prophets, etc. All of this was fulfilled in the years just before the total destruction of Jerusalem. This period is known as, "The War of the Jews," which lasted three and half years, and then the end came.

[1] *Daniel 9:27, 12:11*

Before the Romans began the final and greatest siege of the city, the disciples were warned that they should run to the mountains just like Jesus had told them. They took shelter in a city called Pella, which King Agrippa offered as a refuge for the Christian community.[2]

All the prophecies given by Jesus about His coming and the end of the age were declared to those whom He was sent to, the Jews.

> *When Jesus went out and departed from the temple, and His disciples came up to show Him the buildings of the temple. And Jesus said to them, "Do you not see all these things? Assuredly, I say to you, not one stone shall be left here upon another, that shall not be thrown down."*
>
> *Now as He sat on the Mount of Olives, the disciples came to Him privately, saying, "Tell us, when will these things be? And what will be the sign of Your coming, (parousia) and of the end of the age (aion)?"*
>
> *Matthew 24:1-3*

Jesus uses the words "parousia"[3] which is the word, "presence" in the Greek, and "aion"[4] which means "age". Jesus was not

---

[2] *Westminster Historical Atlas of the Bible page 62*

[3] *3952 Parousia Strong Concordance. Presence, 34 3952. from the present participle of G3918; a being near, i.e. advent (often, return; specially, of Christ to punish Jerusalem, or finally the wicked); (by implication) physically, aspect:—coming, presence. Strong's Biblical Concordance Translation*

3918 (including its various forms); to be near, i.e. at hand; neuter present participle (singular) time being, or (plural) property:—come, × have, be here, + lack, (be here) present. Strong's Biblical Concordance Translation

[4] *165 an age Strong's Biblical Concordance Translation*

talking about coming in a physical body to destroy Jerusalem. Instead He was talking about coming in the clouds with His glorious presence bringing the great judgment which would be very visible.

"The disciples were asking when the end of "aion" would be, or the Moses era, which Jesus had just prophesied would occur.

The Jewish people recognized two ages-the one in which they lived at the time (under the Law), and *the coming age* or the age of the Messiah. A common Jewish conception, which appears many times in the Talmud, is that the coming of the Messiah would end "the age" as it was known and the "coming age" would arrive.

The Jewish people only recognize two ages; the age of the law and the age of the Messiah."[5]

Every time the word "coming" is mentioned in Matthew 24, the words *parousia* and *erchomai* are used. Both refer to a spiritual presence or manifestation.

In the Greek, the word used for physical presence is "*prosopon*," which does not appear in any of these scriptures, referring to the end of the age.
"Parousia" in the Greek means "presence" and Erchomai is the verb "to come," in a grammatical tense referred to as aorist. This tense has no relation to time; it is something that exists or happens eternally.

---

[5] *Raptureless by Jonathan Welton pages 112-113 Published by the author*

The closest thing in English would be the expression made by the Roman Centurion that came to Jesus and asked Him to heal his servant.

The following is an analogy of His authority:

"And I say to this one, 'Go,' and he goes; and to another, 'Come,' and *he comes.*" When does he come? Whenever, it is not future or present. This verb is somewhat like this in the aorist tense. It is an apparition of Christ that happens continuously and in certain points in history, like we will see further in this book, about the judgment He himself decreed, and came to pass in 70 A.D.

(In the section for questions at the end of this book, we explain the meaning of all these words that have to do with the coming of Jesus in His Kingdom.)

In the 24th chapter of Matthew, He first spoke of them seeing: "the sign of the son of man." (Matthew 24:30) Notice, that one thing is a sign and another is a physical manifestation.

This will be clear when we narrate the signs Josephus testified that occurred right before the great fall of Jerusalem. One of them was that they saw the armies of heaven in their chariots on the clouds above the cities. (Chapter 11)

Part of Jesus' ministry was preaching "The great day of the vengeance of our God." This is the day He was referring to in the verses in Matthew, Mark and Luke describing the end.

The Spirit of the Lord God is upon Me, because the Lord has anointed Me to preach good tidings to the poor; He has sent Me to heal the brokenhearted, to proclaim liberty to the captives,

And the opening of the prison to those who are bound; To proclaim the acceptable year of the Lord, ***and the day of vengeance of our God;***

Isaiah 61:1-2a

Jesus spoke directly to those listening, saying:

So you also, when you see all these things, know that it is near—at the doors! Assuredly, I say to you, this generation will by no means pass away till all these things take place. Heaven and earth will pass away, but My words will by no means pass away.

Matthew 24:33-34

The prophecy was made for that generation, and it was related to the fall of Jerusalem and the destruction of the temple.

If He told **them** these things would be fulfilled in **their generation,** it had to be fulfilled in that time. As a matter of fact, it came 37 years after He prophesied. That is also why He said some would not see death before the end came, referring to John who died 30 years after this great judgment.

Also, when the women of Jerusalem cried for Him, He told them:

"...Daughters of Jerusalem, do not weep for Me, but weep for yourselves and for your children. For indeed the days are coming in which they will say, 'Blessed are the barren, wombs that never bore, and breasts which never nursed!'

Then they will begin 'to say to the mountains, "Fall on us!" and to the hills, "Cover us!"'

Luke 23:27-30

Jesus was not talking to women two thousand plus years in the future; He was talking to the ones that would be alive in the judgments from 66 to 70 A.D.

The Early Church knew The End was near

They knew they were in the end times and were awaiting the end as well as the judgment spoken by Jesus over Jerusalem. The apostles prepared this generation to wait for "The day of the Lord."

John knew it:

*Little children, **it is the last hour**; and as you have heard that the Antichrist is coming, even now many antichrists have come, by which we know that it is the last hour.*

1 John 2:18

Peter knew it:

Jesus had spoken to His apostles about how the city would burn and how all the structures of the old priesthood would be removed. What Peter wrote will become very clear when we read later in Josephus' writings about the destruction of Israel by fire. He was worried about the new believers walking in holiness because that day was close. The ministry of Peter was in Jerusalem and even though his writings were copied and sent to Asia Minor, he spoke directly to the Jewish people and the Gentiles who lived there.

But the day of the Lord will come as a thief in the night, in which the heavens will pass away with a great noise, and the elements (structures)[6] will melt with fervent heat; both the earth (territory)[7] and the works that are in it will be burned up.

Therefore, since all these things will be dissolved, what manner of persons ought you to be in holy conduct and godliness, looking for and hastening the coming of the day of God, because of which the heavens will be dissolved, being on fire, and the elements will melt with fervent heat?

2 Peter 3:10-12

---

[6] *The translation in many Bibles says elements, but the Greek word utilized here is "Stoicheon," which means structure or foundation.*

[7] *The Greek word utilized here is "ge," which means a determined territory.*

The Greek word for *elements* is *stoicheion* and it refers to the structures or rudiments of the Mosaic Law. This word is mentioned 5 times in the New Testament.[8]

One of them is:

> *Even so we, when we were children, were in bondage under the elements (stoicheon) of the world.*
>
> *Galatians 4:3*

Peter also affirmed that the end was near in his first letter:

> *But the end of all things is at hand; therefore be serious and watchful in your prayers.*
>
> *1 Peter 4:7*

Paul knew it:

The author of Hebrews, possibly Paul, knowing that day was near, and there would be a horrible tribulation, wrote:

> *For we know Him who said, "Vengeance is Mine, I will repay," says the Lord. And again, "The Lord will judge His people." It is a fearful thing to fall into the hands of the living God.*
>
> **"For yet a little while, And He who is coming will come and will not tarry.**
>
> *Hebrews 10:30-31 & 37*

---

[8] *Galatians 4:3-9; Colossians 2:8, 20; Hebrews 5:12*

He also wrote to the Corinthians:

Now all these things happened to them as examples, and they were written for our admonition, upon whom the ends of the ages have come.

1 Corinthians 10:11

James knew it:

*You also be patient. Establish your hearts, for the coming of the Lord is **at hand**.*

*Do not grumble against one another, brethren, lest you be condemned. Behold, the **Judge is standing at the door**!*

James 5:8-9

The twelve knew it:

When they persecute you in this city, flee to another. For assuredly, I say to you, you will not have gone through the cities of Israel before the Son of Man comes.

Matthew 10:23

Jesus was speaking to the twelve, not to people two thousand years plus in the future.

"Assuredly, I say to you, there are some standing here who shall not taste death till they see the Son of Man coming in His kingdom."

Matthew 16:28

The High Priest heard it:

Jesus declared from that moment on he would see the Lord coming in the clouds.

*Jesus said to him, "It is as you said. Nevertheless, I say to you, **hereafter** you will see the Son of Man sitting at the right hand of the Power, and coming on the clouds of heaven."*

Matthew 26:64

The Page of The Great Confusion

Thousands of years have gone by since the Gospels and the Neo-Testament letters were written. For almost 400 years they remained scattered and hidden to humanity.

In 397 A.D., around the time when the canon of the New Testament was recompiled in the council of Cartago, the Church was already in great decline. The Holy Spirit was completely ignored and the Church had already been transformed into a hierarchical and a Nicolatian system.

By that time, the Catholic Church (the only one that existed at the time) felt a tremendous hatred towards the Jews, since they were directly responsible for the crucifixion of Christ. Another thing that contributed to this hatred was that the Church was romanized, and Rome hated the Jews. That is why they destroyed them.

In an attempt to separate themselves from the Jews, the compilers of the apostolic manuscripts decided that everything that had to do with Christ should not be mixed with the Old Testament.

They decided to begin the New Testament with the Gospels. That way Christianity would be separated from Judaism.

By doing this and placing a page named *"The New Testament"* between Malachi and Matthew, they changed the entire meaning of the interpretation of what Jesus did and said.

Jesus is the beginning and the end, the Alpha and Omega. He is the fulfillment of the entire Old Testament. He is the fulfillment of all justice as well as the Law.

He is the golden seal who closes the Old Testament, who is crowned with the out pouring of the Holy Spirit, prophesied by Joel.

The New Testament should begin when Cornelius receives Salvation in Acts 10. In that moment the work of the Eternal God extends to the world of the Gentiles, and all things are made new. Before this, Jaweh and His Son, Yeshua (Jesus Christ) is the God of the Jews and no one elses.

The Tragedy of the "Out Of Place-Comma"

An example that will help us understand the great tragedy of this badly placed page is the "Out of place-Comma":

The meaning of the phrase, "Let's eat, Grandma," can completely change if it is missing the comma. It would read, "Let's eat Grandma." While humorous, it goes to show how one comma can completely change the meaning of the phrase.

The same occurs with the badly placed New Testament page.

If it is right after Malachi, then it means that Jesus is not the Messiah of Israel that came to fulfill the law. It means He is a Christian Messiah, separated from Israel which did not speak to the Jews, but to the entire world. This would also mean that the promises and the judgments were only for the Church and not for Israel.

This causes us to see the prophecies that He spoke of regarding the end, in the future, and as something that must be fulfilled in our time.

It also causes the Jews to not recognize Jesus as part of their history, but as the Messiah of a new religion called, "Christianity" which is also a Greek word. Therefore, this caused the Jews to not want anything to do with Jesus. THIS IS A GREAT TRAGEDY!

Now, if the page is located in the right place, after Acts 10, Jesus is the Messiah of Israel. He is a part of their history and the fulfillment of all the Law and the prophets. Seeing it this way, that the ministry of Yeshua (Jesus) was only to the Jews, all the prophecies about the end times were fulfilled in His generation.

Then He said to them, "These are the words which I spoke to you while I was still with you, that all things must be fulfilled which were written in the Law of Moses and the Prophets and the Psalms concerning Me." And He opened their understanding, that they might comprehend the Scriptures.

Luke 24:44-45

THE IMPORTANCE OF
KNOWING HISTORY

A Short Story About An Ignorant Man

An ignorant villager, completely unaware of world news lived in the mountains of the Pyrenees in Europe. Even though he lived in the 21st Century, the small village where his house was located lacked the most basic resources of civilization.
One day as he walked the mountains, he found the remains of an old airplane crash site and in it he found a half-burned newspaper. Filled with curiosity, he read, "Hitler declares World War II."

Completely unaware of whom that man was and not knowing anything about World War II, he was greatly frightened when he read the news. While confused, he ran and told his neighbors that they were at war. They then passed on the news to the neighboring towns screaming all over, "We're at war! The end is near! Let's stock up and hide in lairs and caves!"

No one questioned where that information came from and whether it was true or not. They simply assumed that it was right and they should take whatever measures necessary to let as many people know as they could.

Many abandoned their jobs and those who were going to be married, canceled their plans. Young people who wanted to pursue a career gave that up and went into hiding.

As ridiculous as this story is, it is the reality of all those who ignore history.

It is impossible to correctly interpret Old-Testament prophecy, as well as the prophecies of Jesus regarding the end, while ignoring what Israel and the believers experienced in the first century.

The Church and its theologians based all of their conjectures in the few letters we have in the New Testament, leaving out the historical context the early church experienced while under Roman domination.

God allowed other historians and reporters to record historical events other than the writers of the New Testament. They were eye witnesses of the things Israel experienced before the complete destruction of their nation.

Among them, the most well known is a historian named Flavius Josephus.

My purpose in writing these pages is to give you, beloved reader, a summary with extracts from the books of Josephus, to lead you to know the history and fulfillment of all the Biblical prophecies of the "*end times.*"

The most important works he wrote are called, *"The Antiquities of the Jews"* and they comprise 20 books. The second and most relevant to interpret the prophecies of Jesus regarding the end times are called, *"The War of the Jews."*

This last one narrates in detail the Greek-Roman period in Israel's history, and are written in seven books. They describe in great detail the great conflicts found in Israel, the wars against themselves and against the Romans. These wars began in 66 A.D. and culminated three and a half years later in 70 A.D. Israel was completely destroyed with its last fortress refuge being Mazada where the remaining Jews committed a mass suicide.

FLAVIUS JOSEPHUS

Who was *Flavius Josephus?*

The Autobiography of Josephus

Josephus himself describes his origins. He was from a high ranking priestly family; part of the 24 main families that composed Israel's royalty. He was born around 37 or 38 A.D. in the first year of Emperor Caligula's reign.[9]

He writes of himself:

"I was proficient in improving my learning, and appeared to have both great memory and understanding. When I was a child, about fourteen years of age, I was commended by all for the love I had for learning; on which account the high-priests, and principal men of the city, came to me frequently to know my opinion about the accurate understanding of points of the law. And when I was about sixteen years old, I had a mind to discern the several sects that were among us. There were three sects; the first is that of the Pharisees, the second is that of the Sadducees, and the third that of the Essenes."[10] These, represented the right, the left and the extreme left of Jewish legalism respectively.

---

[9] *Roman Emperor that reigned during the first years of Christianity*

[10] *The War of the Jews by Martin Cordero 1557 Edition Editorial Plaza Page 16. Translated from Spanish into English.*

The whole autobiography can be found in some editions of "The war of the Jews" also on line in:http://sacred-texts.com/jud/josephus/autobiog.htm

He became familiar with these three Jewish sects and also went to the desert for three years under the leadership of a hermit called Banos, probably Essenian or related with this sect. Once he felt he had received enough instruction, he left and adhered to Phariseeism.

Josephus and His Allegiance to Rome

In 64 A.D. during Nero's Roman Empire, while Felix was the governor of Judea, Josephus was assigned to travel to Rome. His mission was to request the freeing of two Pharisees who were being held under Roman authority. There, he was presented before Empress Poppaea, Nero's wife, whom he found to be in favor of the Jewish people. She released the imprisoned Jews and bestowed great mercy upon Josephus.

It is believed that this stint in Rome caused Josephus to feel, if not immediate loyalty towards the Romans, at least a strong conviction that the Roman power was invincible, thus defying it was insanity on the part of the Jews.

Soon after returning to Judea, the riot of 66 A.D. broke out and he placed himself at Rome's service after the defeat of Galilee, with his confidence being shattered in advance.

In that year Josephus had led the Galilean defense. Terrorized by the advancement of the Roman legions, the Jewish army deserted and took shelter in a cave where they decided to commit suicide. Josephus arranged it to where he was the last one left and decided to give himself up to the Romans. Taken before Vespasian[11], Josephus predicted that in less than

---

[11] General in charged of the Roman army during the time of Nero's reign.

a year, the general would be the Roman Emperor. This prediction must have given him grace before Vespasian because he pardoned him, influenced by the fact that Josephus had powerful friends in Rome.

Although his true loyalty and love was for his own nation, and as we already mentioned, they considered him a chief noble among them, Josephus also served as a historian and reporter for the Roman people. Later on he became Titus'[12] Jewish counselor.

This allowed him to give reliable testimony of what occurred on both sides.

He was able to learn many details regarding the siege of Jerusalem in the Roman camp. He urged the Jews, in vain, to put an end to the war because he feared for his fellow citizens the consequences of their stubbornness.

Either way, this is a man who knew how to write well in both Aramaic and Greek. Scholars regret that he did not provide more details regarding the sources he used for his work, but being an eye-witness speaks volumes regarding his experience. Although we should point out that he is more of an apologist than a historian, since he deliberately accumulated facts related to his special interests.

Undoubtedly Josephus' works are of immeasurable historical value, especially to Christians who may cross-check them with the inspired accounts we have in the New and even Old Testament.

---

[12] *Son of Vespacian, and General of the army, while his father was Emperor of Rome.*

After the taking and plundering of the Holy City (in 70 A.D.), Josephus believed it would be sensible to escape the likely vengeance of some of his exiled patriots, who criticized his conduct, so he followed Titus to Rome. That is when his Roman citizenship was grantedand he took the name Flavius. This was appropriate for the notable Jew, who frequented the treaty between Vespasian and Titus (Roman Emperors of the Flavian Dynasty).

THE DESTRUCTION OF JERUSALEM AND THE TEMPLE IN HISTORY

It is important to place the reader in the historical background of the powers that subjugated Judea right before the first century. This will allow the reader to see what was happening, what the circumstances were and which characters led Israel into its decline. We will then delve into the wars of the Jews and the incidents that led to its total destruction.

Jerusalem Was Taken Several Times in History

Before the birth of Jesus, Jerusalem had been destroyed several times. Not all the prophecies that spoke of the destruction of Jerusalem refer to the final devastation of 70 A.D.
There were prophets that referred to the previous destructions and reconstructions of the different temples that were built after Solomon's temple.

Josephus writes about these different destructions:
"It was first destroyed by the king of Babylon after 1360 years, eight months and six days after it was built. Then the King of Egypt, Asocheus and then Antiochus Epiphanes of Pompeii (which partially destroyed the Temple), then Sosius and Herod took it and conserved it." (Herod built the last temple).

"The first to build it or establish it was a powerful Canaanite named Mechizedech, which means a "just man" in the language of the homeland and it was so; that is why he was the first that served and administered the priesthood for God and as he began to build the Temple, he called the city Jerusalem, because it was called Salem before."

The Destruction of Jerusalem
by King Nebuchadnezzar in Babylon

This destruction was prophesied by Isaiah[13] and Jeremiah.[14]

It happened approximately in the year 586 B.C., on the seventh of Av, which is the fifth month. Nebuzaradan, captain of the guard of Babylon destroyed the Temple which was built by Solomon with much effort. The Bible records this tragic event:

> *And in the fifth month, on the seventh day of the month (which was the nineteenth year of King Nebuchadnezzar king of Babylon), Nebuzaradan the captain of the guard, a servant of the king of Babylon, came to Jerusalem. He burned the house of the Lord and the king's house; all the houses of Jerusalem, that is, all the houses of the great, he burned with fire.*

---

[13] *760 - 700 B.C.*

[14] *650 - 586 B.C.*

The bronze pillars that were in the house of the Lord, and the carts and the bronze Sea that were in the house of the Lord, the Chaldeans broke in pieces, and carried their bronze to Babylon. They also took away the pots, the shovels, the trimmers, the spoons, and all the bronze utensils with which the priests ministered. The firepans and the basins, the things of solid gold and solid silver, the captain of the guard took away. The two pillars, one Sea, and the carts, which Solomon had made for the house of the Lord, the bronze of all these articles was beyond measure.

2 Kings 25:8-9 & 13-16

Our holy and beautiful temple, where our fathers praised You, Is burned up with fire;

Isaiah 64:11

That beautiful Temple that was filled with the glory of God was reduced to rubble and to the shame of the people, 403 years after its construction. During four centuries God put up with the sin of the Jews until their wickedness brought their ruin.

During the Babylonian captivity there were prophets that prophesied the rebuilding of the Temple. They were Ezekiel, Haggai and Zachariah.

They referred to the will of God to rebuild the Temple once again before the coming of the Messiah. Jesus came among many other things, to destroy the old system of the Temple and in order for this to occur, it needed to be rebuilt. It was destroyed and was rebuilt twice before the coming of the Son of God.

The Rebuilding of The Temple during the Medo-Persian Empire

After the return of the captivity of Babylon, during the Medo-Persian Empire, the Temple in Jerusalem was rebuilt, approximately in the year 417 B.C. For the Jews it was a joyous celebration because they could serve God in the Temple again. This Temple was much smaller and plain compared to the one Solomon had built. This is the Temple Zerubbabel built, assisted by Cyrus, King of Persia.

> *The hands of Zerubbabel have laid the foundation of this temple; His hands shall also finish it. Then you will know*
>
> *That the Lord of hosts has sent Me to you.*
>
> *For who has despised the day of small things? For these seven rejoice to see the plumb line in the hand of Zerubbabel.*
>
> *They are the eyes of the Lord, which scan to and fro throughout the whole earth.*
>
> *Zachariah 4:9-10*

The people continued disobeying God and so a new yoke and a new destruction came.

Judea Under the Greek and Roman Empires, II and I B.C.

By the second century before Christ, the Greek Empire dominated a great part of the known world, including Israel.

Two large factions among the Greeks fought over control of the Empire. One was Ptolomeu and the other was Antiochus Epiphanes.

This last man was a perverse tyrant that brought great destruction over Israel.

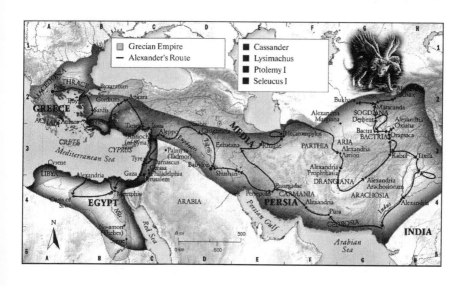

Fig. 1 — Map of the Empire of Greece

C1. The Domination of Greece

Antiochus Epiphanes was a Grecian Emperor of the Seleucid Dynasty (central part) between the years 212 and 163 B.C.

Back then the chiefs of the Jews, who represented the sects of the Pharisees, were in great conflict with one another. In the meantime Antiochus Epiphanes organized an expedition against Jerusalem.

Josephus, being a historian, writes regarding these times:

"And came upon the Jews with a great army, and took their city by force, and slew a great multitude of those that favored Ptolemy, and sent out his soldiers to plunder them without mercy. He also robbed the temple, and put a stop to the practice of offerings as a daily sacrifice for three years and six months.[15]
Now Antiochus was not satisfied with his unexpected taking of the city, or with its pillage, or with the great slaughter he had made there; but being overcome with his violent passions, and remembering what he had suffered during the siege, he compelled the Jews to dissolve the laws of their country, and to keep their infants uncircumcised, and to sacrifice swine's flesh upon the altar; which they all opposed, and those who stood up to defend their Law, were put to death."[16]

According to the *Book of the Maccabees*, Antiochus promulgated several religious type ordinances: He tried to suppress the worship to Yahveh and tried to establish worship

---

[15] *Josephus, War of the Jews Book 1 Chapter 1 page 10*

[16] *Josephus, War of the Jews Book 1 Chapter 1 page 10*

to Greek gods. However, the Jewish Priest Mattathias and his two sons called Maccabees were able to rally the people against him and they overthrew him. The Jewish festival of Hanukkah commemorates this event.

C2. The Roman Empire

The last stage of Roman history was referred to as an Empire in which Rome was governed by emperors. They established an absolute government where all power was set upon them; political, military, religious and administrative. This stage started in 29 B.C. with the reign of Augustus (Octavius) and ended with the reign of Romulus Augustulus in the year 476 A.D., due to the barbaric invasions of the fifth century.

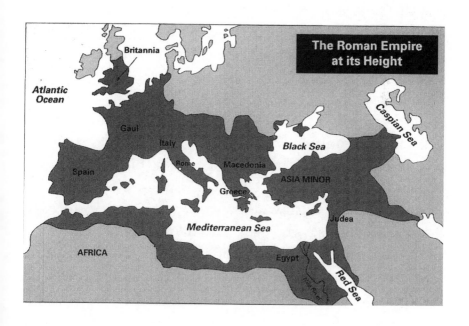

Fig. 2 — The Domination of The Roman Empire

Pompeius Magnus

In the year 63 B.C. Rome conquered the Empire of Greece. There was a politician and Roman general called Pompeius. who was one of the ones who took Jerusalem and desecrated the temple, leaving it quite damaged. He then tried to find grace among the Jews by promoting among them the restoration of the daily sacrifice.

Flavius Josephus narrates in, "Antiquities of the Jews," the events that took place during that siege.

"Of the Jews, twelve thousand fell, but of the Romans very few... and no small damage was caused to the Temple itself, which, in the former ages, had been inaccessible, and seen by no one.

Pompey went into the temple with many others and they all saw what was unlawful for any man to see besides the high priests. Yet Pompey did not touch anything on account of his respect for their religion; and at this point , he acted in a manner that was worthy of his virtue. *The next day* he gave the order to those who were in charge of the Temple to cleanse it, and to bring what offerings the law required to God. He also restored the high priesthood to Hyrcanus, of the Pharisees sect."[17]

---

[17] *Josephus, Antiquities of the Jews, Book 14, Chapter 4*

Fig. 3 — Pompeius and the Dead Inside the Temple

"Herod the Great," King of Judea

Herod the Great became the king of Judea in 40 B.C. At that time, the building had suffered considerably, due to natural disintegration as well as hostile military attacks.

In an attempt to obtain the favor of the Jews, Herod was determined to reconstruct the temple. The work started in approximately 25 B.C. and required a lot of work and money. It was filled with splendor. That is why it was called, "Herod's Temple" or Second Temple. This is the temple where the Lord Jesus Christ drove out the money changers. It had been turned into a den of thieves and a business center. The people were still far from the will of God, and that is why Jesus prophesied against the temple:

> Then Jesus went out and departed from the temple, and His disciples came up to show Him the buildings of the temple. And Jesus said to them, "Do you not see all these things? Assuredly, I say to you, not one stone shall be left here upon another, that shall not be thrown down.
>
> *Matthew 24:1-2*

As we will see in the coming pages, this prophecy was fulfilled in 70 A.C., when Titus, the Roman General, invaded Jerusalem and destroyed the Temple in Av 9 of the Jewish calendar. Oddly enough, this was exactly 2 days after the 656th anniversary of the destruction of Solomon's temple by the Babylonians. Yet, some among them assured it was the same day.

Who Ruled in Rome During the 1st Century?

Caligula, Claudius and Nero of the Claudian Dynasty

During the time of Jesus, Caligula ruled as the Emperor of Rome and governed over Judea, Herod Agrippa I. This emperor was followed by Claudius Cesar and he was followed by Nero who set Rome on fire the first time. These three rulers violently persecuted Christians and threw them to the lions, crucified them and burned them alive in the Roman Circus, but they weren't the only ones.

Non-Dynasty Emperors

At the time of Nero's death in the winter of 68 A.D., three more emperors governed, one right after the other in a one year time span, for very short periods of time. They were Galba, Otton and Vitellius. It could be considered only one government that ruled during the civil wars.

Vespasian and Titus, of The Flavian Destiny

Later on Vespasian was crowned as Emperor. He was the general of Nero's army. He ruled the Empire during the destruction of Jerusalem in 70 A.D. and his son, Titus, was the General of his armies.

It is important to know these names because it will help us understand how history unraveled and how the prophecy was fulfilled.

Jesus in His glory, in approximately[18] 67 A.D., prophesied in the Book of Revelation. He was warning His people of the events that were soon about to take place. Jesus wanted to encourage them and give them understanding of the great destruction that would come upon Jerusalem and all of Judea through the Roman Empire.

Here is the mind which has wisdom: The seven heads are seven mountains on which the woman sits. There are also seven kings. Five have fallen, one is, and the other has not yet come. And when he comes, he must continue a short time. The beast that was, and is not, is himself also the eighth, and is of the seven, and is going to perdition.

Revelation 17:9-11

The beast symbolized the Roman Empire, personalized in Nero, which began the destruction of the Jewish nation in 66 A.D., by sending General Vespasian to siege Jerusalem and take the nation. Here it is very important to place Jesus' prophecies in the timeframe of what was about to happen.

The Roman Empire was made up of approximately 20 nations that did not get along with each other. (See fig. 2) This caused it to be a mixture of iron and clay, just as Daniel prophesied to King Nebuchadnezzar when he had the dream of the great image.

---

[18] *Some believe that the book of Revelation was written in 95 A.D., but that is incorrect since in Chapter 11 the destruction of the city and the temple is predicted, and this happened in 70 A.D.*

This image represented the four empires that conquered Israel and corrupted it: Babylon, Persia, Greece and Rome. The feet symbolized the Roman Empire and "the rock,"who was Jesus, would come to destroy all structures of accumulated corruption for seven-hundred years. When this structure fell, The Kingdom of God would be established and Jesus would rule with His saints.[19]

> *As you saw iron mixed with ceramic clay, they will mingle with the seed of men; but they will not adhere to one another, just as iron does not mix with clay. And in the days of these kings the God of heaven will set up a kingdom which shall never be destroyed; and the kingdom shall not be left to other people; it shall break in pieces and consume all these kingdoms, and it shall stand forever.*
>
> *Daniel 2:43-44*

Now then, going back to the scripture of the eight kings in Revelation 17, let us see who these kings were:

In the next graphic, we see the 5 kings of the Julius-Claudius dynasty. Among them was Nero, who is described as the "one who is." (Nero was the emperor in 67 A.D., who *Jesus prophesied about in the book of Revelation.*)

This was followed by the period of the four "non-dynasty" emperors during the civil wars in 69 A.D. These could be considered the sixth one. At the end of that year the Flavian

---

[19] *Daniel 2: 36-45*

Dynasty surged with Vespasian, the seventh king. He was succeeded by his son Titus, who inherited the Empire from his father. Being the son of Vespasian, he was the eighth, while at the same time, the *seventh*, because of his bloodline.

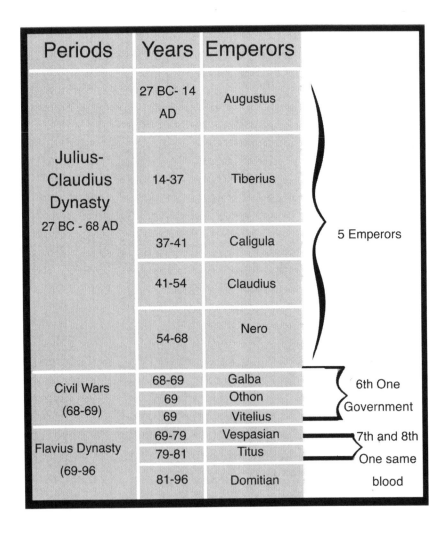

Periods	Years	Emperors	
Julius-Claudius Dynasty 27 BC - 68 AD	27 BC- 14 AD	Augustus	5 Emperors
	14-37	Tiberius	
	37-41	Caligula	
	41-54	Claudius	
	54-68	Nero	
Civil Wars (68-69)	68-69	Galba	6th One Government
	69	Othon	
	69	Vitelius	
Flavius Dynasty (69-96	69-79	Vespasian	7th and 8th
	79-81	Titus	One same blood
	81-96	Domitian	

Fig. 4 — Roman Emperors of The First Century

CHAPTER 5

THE SECTS AND THE MOST IMPORTANT CHARACTERS IN THE WARS AMONG THE JEWS

The Jewish Sects and The Political Movements That Provoked The Conflicts

Israel was divided into three religious sects: The sects of the Pharisees, the Sadducees and the Essenes. Aside from these, we will see a very important political movement that rose up called the Zealots.

We will also present the Jewish tyrants who rose up against the Romans, and for this reason were considered by many to be like messiahs. They along with their helpers, caused the internal destruction or civil war within Israel.

The Three Sects Of Judaism

The Sadducees

"They were the right of Jewish legalism. They were recruited among nobility, priests and intellectuals. They were followers of Hellenism and did not believe in a special mission of sacred character on behalf of the Jews as a result of Abraham's calling. They did not allow faith in the resurrection of the dead or the angelology of the Pharisees and had no sympathy for Messiahnism."

"We frequently find them joined to the priests and scribes as confederate enemies of Jesus Christ and even though it seems illogical, some of the priests belonged to this skeptical sect. They were the realistic politicians who thought it was a utopia the idea of a Jewish world domination. They formed a small, but greatly influential minority in the times of Christ."

"They disagreed among each other regarding fierce customs and did not think highly of foreigners. They were actually very inhumane towards them."

The Pharisees

"The Pharisees, on the other hand, belonged to the middle class and formed a strictly Jewish, legalistic party. They believed that the Jews had to be a holy people, dedicated to God and they believed in The Kingdom of God. They stood out in the synagogue where the people received instruction from the most educated among them and were admired by the people for this."

"They tended to attribute what ever happened in life both to God and to fortune. They said that doing good or bad was in the hands of men, but that good fortune helped them in everything. They also said that all souls are incorruptible, but that only the good ones pass on to other bodies and the bad ones are tormented with pleadings and torments that never end."[20]

Pharisees loved one another and showed goodness to one another.

Saul of Tarsus was one of the few sincere Pharisees and was chosen by the Lord.

The Essenes

"As far as the Essenes, we know they formed a small religious minority and lived in communities very similar to the friars of our time, but their ideals were as much political as religious. They practiced very strict humanitarianism; a true kingdom of God without restrictions from the State and without civil law."

"The Essenes considered themselves the eschatological people of God because they believed that fulfilling the law would bring about divine intervention in the form of a war that would put an end to all the governments of the earth. Therefore, in order to be admitted into this sect they required an apprenticeship of several years, surrendering of private property and in many cases, giving up marriage.

[20] *Page 111 Paragraph 14*

Once the new member was accepted, he would work in agriculture and manual labor, but above all he would dedicate himself to the studying of Scripture. They had community assemblies and practiced daily ablutions and conscience examinations."

The Movements of political revolt and the false messiahs who rose up

The Zealots

The Zealots were a political-nationalist movement in the first century and were founded by Judas of Galilee, soon after the birth of Jesus. The name refers to the zeal its members had towards Yahweh.

They were the most violent sect of Judaism of their time, frequently clashing with others, such as the Pharisees and Sadducees, whom they accused of having a "zeal for money." The term zealot has come to be known as synonymous, in several languages, to intransigent or radical militants.

Some historians consider them the first terrorist groups in history, since they utilized the homicide of civilians who collaborated with the Roman government to dissuade others from doing the same thing. Within the zealot movement, a radicalized faction known as **Sicarios** distinguished themselves, due to their virulence and sectarianism.

Their objective was a Judea, independent from the Roman Empire through armed warfare. We will see this develop in these pages.

Due to the great fall of Jerusalem in 70 A.D., they occupied the Fortress of Masada, which served as the last Zealot refuge. Three years later they committed mass suicide, in this place, refusing to surrender to the Romans.

John of Giscala

For false christs and false prophets will rise and show great signs and wonders to deceive, if possible, even the elect.

Matthew 24:24

Upon the death of Judas the Galilean, founder of the Zealot movement, a new leader rose up, named John of Giscala. Due to the idea held by the Pharisees that the Messiah would deliver them from their oppressors, the Romans; they considered John their Messiah due to the fierceness and cruelty with which he fought Rome.

Josephus writes regarding him:

"It was John, the son of a certain man named Levi that drew them to rebel and encouraged them in it. He was a cunning, archaic man, and had a temper that could put on various shapes; very rash in expecting great things and very sagacious in bringing about what he hoped for. It was known to everybody that he was fond of war, in order to thrust himself into authority; and the seditious part of the people were under his management."[21]

---

[21] *The Wars of the Jews, Book IV Chapter 2 page 201*

Simon Bari Giora

"At the time a new blood thirsty, enlightened man by the name of Simon Bar Giora, also known as Simon Ben Kojba managed to join together a strong group of discontent Jews and organized a party of violent evildoers.

His name went down in history when the Tana Rabbi Akiva Ben Iosef, a wise rabbi and influential person in the Sanhedrin, allowed him to take on the name, "Bar Kokeba ("*Son of a Star*" in Aramaic), referencing the Biblical verse in Numbers 24:17, *"A Star shall come out of Jacob"*). Thus, Akiva declared Ben Kojba as the authentic *Messiah* that would deliver the Jewish people from its oppressors.[22]

In the midst of the war against Rome, the people of Israel were bleeding to death in useless civil wars. In Jerusalem the Zealots were killing one another and were divided among themselves into two groups, those who fought with John and those with Simon.

When Simon Bar Giora arrived in Jerusalem, he faced John of Giscala in a horrible massacre, which lasted many days. Thousands of innocent Jews died, caught up between both groups. Both would burn up each other's supplies which could have helped feed the enormous population trapped by the Roman siege."

---

[22] *Article: http://www.simpletoremember.com/articles/a/the_bar_kochba_revolt/*

The Dispersed Jews throughout Asia and Europe

It is important to understand that the Jews were not concentrated within Israel during the times of Jesus or in the first century. During the wars of the Jews, Rome launched a strong attack, conquering every place where there were Jewish settlements.

These Jewish settlements were the ones Jesus referred to as the nations that would be judged. Also, the term "Gentile nations," was given to the kingdoms under the yoke of Rome, who formed the existing world in those days.

As an example of this the Jewish nations came together at the feast of Pentecost, when the Holy Spirit was poured out. The dispersed Jews referred to themselves as nations and as such they had gone to Jerusalem to celebrate the feast. They marveled when they saw the disciples speaking the tongues of their nations.

> *Then they were all amazed and marveled, saying to one another, "Look, are not all these who speak Galileans? And how is it that we hear, each in our own language in which we were born? Parthians and Medes and Elamites, those dwelling in Mesopotamia, Judea and Cappadocia, Pontus and Asia, Phrygia and Pamphylia, Egypt and the parts of Libya adjoining Cyrene, visitors from Rome, both Jews and proselytes, Cretans and Arabs — we hear them speaking in our own tongues the wonderful works of God."*
>
> *Acts 2:7-11*

They were all Jewish. The Gentiles did not travel to Jerusalem to celebrate the Jewish feasts.

When Jesus prophesied that nation would rise up against nation, He was referring to the Jewish nations, which fought against one another in the wars of the Jews.

When He spoke of judging the nations in the valley of decision, He was referring to the Jews. His prophecy was directed towards Israel and the end that was near.

As we delve into the wars that we will be studying, we will see horrific situations of brother rising up against brother, nation against nation, attacking one another.

> *For nation will rise against nation, and kingdom against kingdom. And there will be famines, pestilences, and earthquakes in various places. All these are the beginning of sorrows.*
>
> *Matthew 24:7-8*

NOTES
Additional Details regarding
the Formation of These Jewish Nations

King Nebuchadnezzar deported large groups of Jews into Babylon between the years 605 and 587 B.C. Despite Cyrus' edict, the majority of the exiled preferred to remain in Babylon due to the economic and agricultural conditions being favorable towards them. Gradually, from 400 B.C. to 200 A.D., they occupied several nations in Europe.

"Josephus describes Syria as the country with the highest percentage of Jewish inhabitants, probably due to its close proximity to Israel. Particularly, there were important Jewish centers in the capital, Antioch as well as in Damascus and Apamea. A great number of Jews lived in Syria and Asia Minor where the Jewish settlements were encouraged by the policies of Seleucides kings (Greek Empire) which governed large areas in Asia Minor. There were also many Jews in several islands in the Eastern Mediterranean. Many lived in Crete, Delos, Paros, Melas, Euboea and other islands."

" ...there were Jews in the urban centers in Greece and Macedonia... According to the Acts of the Apostles; there were Jewish communities in Thessalonica, in the Macedonian cities of Philippi and Berea as well as the well-known cities of Athens and Corinth. Inscriptions still remaining show evidence of the existence of Jewish colonies in several places in the Peloponnese (Greece)."[23]

---

[23] (Jewish Encyclopedia s.v. "Diaspora," 6: 10-11.)

THE WARS OF THE JEWS
BY FLAVIUS JOSEPHUS

When I read these 7 books, I was perplexed at seeing the accuracy of the words Jesus used to prophecy the destruction of Jerusalem and the end of the era. Everything was vividly narrated by Josephus.

The books begin with a prologue that summarizes the development of all the wars until the final defeat in Judea.

During 66 A.D. there were major conflicts in Judea. The nation was divided and controlled by John of Giscala, leader of the Zealots and there were revolts everywhere.
Rome attempted to control these internal wars to no avail. In the end these insurrections led to the total destruction of Jerusalem in 70 A.D. The Roman army simply gave the last stab.

That is how Jesus predicted it 37 years earlier. These wars were signs the disciples had to look out for to know the end was near.

And you will hear of wars and rumors of wars. See that you are not troubled; for all these things must come to pass, but the end is not yet.

Matthew 24:6

FLAVIUS JOSEPHUS' PROLOGUE OF THE SEVEN BOOKS OF THE WARS OF THE JEWS (EXRACTS)

"Because the war the Romans waged against the Jews is the greatest our age and times witnessed and the greatest we have ever heard of, regarding city against city and people against people."[24]

"The imprisoned captives in the entire war reached ninety-seven thousand and those that died totaled one-million, one-hundred thousand, (plus women and children). They were Jews, but not all were from Jerusalem because they had come for the Passover Feast. They were suddenly closed into the war and the Roman's siege.

First, because they were closed in, they suffered great pestilence and then the hunger came."[25]

For then there will be great tribulation, such as has not been since the beginning of the world until this time, no, nor ever shall be.

Matthew 24:21

---

[24] *Wars of the Jews, Joseph's Prologue. I have translated some into more contemporary English to make it easier to understand. Also, the text in parenthesis is added to help the reader identify the place or a certain character.*

[25] *War of the Jews Preface page 5*

And there will be great earthquakes in various places, and famines and pestilences; and there will be fearful sights and great signs from heaven.

Luke 21:11

"The Jews, earnest in age but lacking judgment, seeing they flourished no less in riches than in strength, had such a terrible sense of time that they arose hoping to possess the East, (occupied by Rome) and were then very frightened."

"The Jews thought that all those that were on the other side of the Euphrates would rise up against the Romans as well (in the Eastern Empire). The Romans were bothered by the British, their neighbors, and the Germans as well. The universe was full of discord after Nero's Empire. Taking advantage of the times and major revolts, many pretended to rise up with the Empire. Hoping to have a better gain, the armies wanted to mix it all up."[26]

"Witness to it all was Emperor Titus Caesar who gained it all. He saw how everything was destroyed because of the discord among the naturals (the Jews) along with the great tyrants that had risen up, and how they forced the Romans to light everything on fire and burning the sacred temple. He always had mercy on the people but he was prohibited from doing what he wanted for them due to the seditious rebels. Many times he even extended the siege longer than necessary to avoid destroying the city and allow the authors of this great war to repent."

---

[26] *Wars of the Jews, Preface page 6*

"In the end if we compared all the adversities and destruction that have occurred since the creation of the universe to the destruction of the Jews, all the others are inferior and less in volume."

"But I will take the beginning of my story where they, along with our prophets ended. I will tell as diligently and at length as I can about the war that occurred in my time. I will speak of the war that began twelve years into Nero's Empire and I will speak of all of the events and all the damage that took place due to Cestius[27] and of all that was gained by the Jews at the beginning. I will tell of how they strengthened their people, and of how Nero, because of the damage brought upon by Cestius, fearing the state of the universe, made Vespasian general captain. He then entered through Judea with his oldest son and with a great army of Romans, killing multitudes of people throughout Galilee. I will tell of how he took the cities by force as well as others which surrendered."

"In speaking of this I will faithfully include the truth of what I've seen and suffered; I will not hold back from telling of the misery and misfortune because I am telling it to those that know of it and saw it."

---

[27] *Cestius Gallus (67 A.D.) was the son of a consul in Ancient Rome and he himself was consul suffectus in 42 A.D.*

He was Legate in Syria en 63 A.D. or 65 A.D. He marched to Judea in 66 A.D. in an attempt to restore peace at the beginning of the Great Jewish Rebellion. He was successful in the victorious Beit She'arim in the Jezreel Valley, the headquarters of the Great Sanhedrin (the supreme Jewish religious tribunal) at the time, but he was not able to take Jerusalem.

"Then, after the Jewish state was demolished, Nero died and Vespasian, having made his way towards Jerusalem was detained due to the empire and left for Egypt (to the funeral). He took his son Titus with him. I will also speak of the mutilations and revolts that took place in Rome, and how Vespasian was declared Emperor by the people of war, against his will. I will tell of how the Jews were involved in domestic revolts and seditions. I will describe how they were subjected to tyrants and how these tyrants were involved in discords and great seditions. Going back to Titus, after Egypt, he came against Judea twice and entered the lands along with his army. I will speak of the many times the city was afflicted while he was present."

"Then I will declare the cruelty of the Jewish tyrants that rose up in Judea against their own and the humanity and clemency of the Romans with foreigners. Titus, wanting to keep the city and conserve the temple, compelled the rebels to seek and ask for peace and harmony."

"I will describe in detail the wounds and misfortune of all the people and how much they suffered sometimes due to war and others times due to seditions and revolts as well as hunger and how in the end they were imprisoned. I will not stop telling of the deaths of those that attempted to flee and the punishment and torture the captives experienced. I will tell of how the temple was burned against Caesar's will and how the many treasures and riches perished due to the fire as well as the slaughter and destruction of the main city, which all of Judea depended on."

"I will tell of the marvelous signs and wonders that took place right before the horrendous events and of how the tyrants were captured and imprisoned. I will describe how the Romans resumed their victory and demolished from the root all the Jewish strongholds and defenses and how as Titus conquered all of these lands, he reduced them to his mandate, and of his return to Italy and his triumph."

"Everything I have said I have written in seven books for those that desire to know the truth. I will begin my story in the same order I have told it in summarized form."

Israel would be destroyed by the Roman army and dispersed throughout the nations. This is the story of its destruction.

They will fall by the sword and will be taken as prisoners to all the nations. *Jerusalem will be trampled on by the Gentiles until the times of the Gentiles are fulfilled.*[28]

Luke 21:24

---

[28] *The word used here is Kairos, which implies the opportunity of the gentiles, as opposed to Cronos as if to imply measurable time.*

The Beginning of The Destruction of Jerusalem

The Beginning of the Wars

The first revolt began in 66 A.D. in Caesarea. After winning a legal dispute before the judges, the Greeks provoked a fight in the Jewish neighborhood and the Roman garrison did not intervene. The rage of the Jews grew when they found out the Roman procurator of Judea, Gessius Florus, had stolen money from the treasury of the Temple.

Also, in an act of defiance, the son of the High Priest, Eleazer Ben Ananias **stopped the prayers and the sacrifices in the Temple** in honor of the Roman Emperor and gave the order to attack the Roman garrison that was in Jerusalem. The governor of Galilee, as well as the governor of Judea (Herod Agrippa II) fled while Cestius Gallus (Roman general in Syria) put together an important force to march to Jerusalem and suffocate the rebels.

The Jews managed to fend off Cestius Gallus' forces in Beth Horon and forced him to leave, having killed 6,000 Legionaries.

Prophet Daniel clearly describes this episode and what would be the end of Israel as well as the things that would occur as a sign to those with understanding. It paralleled what Jesus prophesied about the end.

> *Many shall be purified, made white, and refined, but the wicked shall do wickedly; and none of the wicked shall understand, but the wise shall understand. "And from the time that the daily sacrifice is taken away, and the abomination of desolation is set up, there shall be one thousand two hundred and ninety days.*
>
> *Daniel 12:10-11*

The 1,290 days are equal to three and a half years. This is how long the wars lasted, up until the final destruction of Jerusalem, as well as the end of the antique priestly system.

Some Scholars place this 1,290 years from the resurrection of Jesus in 31 A.D. to the death of Stephen in 34 A.D.

The important fact here is that either of these interpretations swirl around the generation that Jesus prophesied to, the Jews of His time.

> *And forces shall be mustered by him, and they shall defile the sanctuary fortress; then they shall take away the daily sacrifices, and place there the abomination of desolation.*

Those who do wickedly against the covenant he shall corrupt with flattery; but the people who know their God shall be strong, and carry out great exploits.

And those of the people who understand shall instruct many; yet for many days they shall fall by sword and flame, by captivity and plundering.

Now when they fall, they shall be aided with a little help; but many shall join with them by intrigue.

And some of those of understanding shall fall, to refine them, purify them, and make them white, until the time of the end; because it is still for the appointed time.

Daniel 11:31-35

The Romans had a deep rooted, irrational hatred against the Jews and the Christian Church; the majority of which were converted Jews.

Nero, who was the Roman Emperor in Rome, would crucify or throw into the lions den to be devoured, anyone who converted to Christ. There were a great amount of martyrs. On the other hand, General Cestius and then General Vespasian (who would later become emperor) seized and fiercely attacked the cities in Israel.

Vespasian, supported by his son Titus, had already taken several cities, Yodfat, Tiberias, Gamala, Caesarea of the sea, Gadara and others, by the time he reached Gischala. "There he conquered Galilee in the way of the Romans, destroying entire cities, executing hundreds of thousands of men and selling the women and children as slaves. Rome could not be messed with, but it was too late for the Jews to understand this."[29]

The Jews and the Christians, those who were left alive and managed to escape, would go from city to city, fleeing for their lives and preaching the Gospel.

When they persecute you in this city, flee to another. For assuredly, I say to you, you will not have gone through the cities of Israel before the Son of Man comes.

Matthew 10:23

The Wars Continue

1. John of Gischala flees with the People towards Jerusalem

Flavius Josephus describes the escape:

"The Roman's attitude provoked such terror in the Jewish cities that the majority of the people surrendered without opposition, while thousands and thousands of Jews, terrified, fled towards Jerusalem led by John of Gischala. Meanwhile, Vespasian sent his son Titus, with a squadron of thousands of men on horses, to follow them and kill them."

---

[29] *War of the Jews by Flavio Josephus Resume of Book 3 and Chapter 1 of book IV from pages 159 - 200*

"Now in the night time, when John saw there were no Roman guards about the city, he seized the opportunity directly, and taking with him not only the armed men who were with him, but a considerable number of those who had little to do, together with their families, fled to Jerusalem."[30]

The women and children followed about 20 stadiums behind. As they fled, many fell andothers were fighting amongst themselves over who else would flee, stepping one over another. "There was a miserable destruction made of the women and the children, while some of them took courage to call their husbands and kinsmen back, and so beseech them with the bitterest lamentations, to stay for them; but John's exhortation, who cried out to them to save themselves, and fly away, prevailed. He cried out that they should flee because if the Romans captured them, aside from taking them captive they would also be killed. All those that fled scattered themselves as much as they could depending on their strength." [31]

When John arrived in Jerusalem with the men of war that followed him, he made arrangements with the Zealots who were there and made the Temple his refuge and center of operations.

Meanwhile, Titus killed two thousand men that fled and he took three thousand women and children captive.[32]

---

[30] *War of the Jews Book IV Chapter 2, Page 202*

[31] *War of the Jews Book IVChapter 2, Page 202*

[32] *War of the Jews Book IV Chapter 4, Page 212-213 I used the Spanish version translation since is easier to read.*

2. The Beginning of The Destruction

"All of the people in Jerusalem were broken-hearted with the arrival of John and they would ask all those who fled how it had gone for them and what slaughter had taken place. All they could do was weep, for they clearly understood the penalty they had suffered."[33]

"Hearing about what the captives had suffered and endured caused everyone to be sad and perturbed. They thought this was a great argument to believe their own destruction. John was not ashamed of having left some behind, and would even go everywhere inciting everyone to war, convincing them of the weakness of the enemy and flaunting their own strength. He would deceive the simple ones who lacked understanding in matters of war. He would tell them that even if the Romans fled, they could never enter through Jerusalem's walls since their engines and battering rams were worn down by the damage caused in so many battles. He would corrupt a great number of young people with his words, but all of the older and more prudent people cried for the city that was pretty much lost, knowing full well what was about to happen."

"There was confusion among the people. The farmers and rustic people in the neighboring areas of Jerusalem rose up and began to clash and fight amongst one another."

---

[33] *Book 4 Chapter 3 page 204. Translation by the author to modern English.*

"All of the cities were in revolt and were clashing with one another. Whenever the Romans let up on their fighting against them, they would begin to kill one another. There was a large and cruel dispute among those that wanted peace and those that loved war and sought it. This discord would rise up within their homes and then the closest of friends were in discord and each one would join with their relatives and with those they intended to defend. That is how all of the people were divided into towns and they would rebel."[34]

Jews and believers (who were Jewish as well) were all living this great conflict, just as Jesus had spoken.

And then many will be offended, will betray one another, and will hate one another. Then many false prophets will rise up and deceive many. And because lawlessness will abound, the love of many will grow cold. But he who endures to the end shall be saved. (And this gospel of the kingdom will be preached in all the world as a witness to all the nations, and then the end will come.)[35]

Matthew 24:10-13

Do you suppose that I came to give peace on earth? I tell you, not at all, but rather division. For from now on five in one house will be divided: three against two, and two against three. Father will be divided against son and son

---

[34] *Idem*

[35] *This last part of the verse is missing in most original manuscripts.*

against father, mother against daughter and daughter against mother, mother-in-law against her daughter-in-law and daughter-in-law against her mother-in-law."

Then He also said to the multitudes, "Whenever you see a cloud rising out of the west, immediately you say, 'A shower is coming'; and so it is. And when you see the south wind blow, you say, 'There will be hot weather'; and there is. Hypocrites! You can discern the face of the sky and of the earth, but how is it you do not discern this time?

Luke 12:51-56

"The natural ones (Jews) began to rob and commit larceny amongst the mobs throughout the land. Their cruelty and injustice did not differ from that of the Romans. Those who were being destroyed by them preferred to be killed in the hands of the Romans, since it seemed less cruel compared to the suffering inflicted on them by the natural ones."[36]

"This city (Jerusalem) was not ruled by anyone in particular among the Jews. They would embrace anyone who wanted to live there. Upon seeing so many people enter, the naturals thought they were coming to assist them. This brought great disgrace in the end since many useless people who provided no benefit only stayed to use up the supplies and sustenance of the city."[37]

"Besides the war, this caused hunger to break out which brought with it even more sedition and revolts. Many thieves

---

[36] *War of the Jews Book IV Chapter 3 page 206*

[37] *Paraphrased Summary War of the Jews Book IV Chapter 3*

came from outside and got together with those that were already within the walls. They were even crueler and would not cease to commit all kind of evil deeds, even the biggest and most horrendous ones.

"They were not happy with just stealing and stripping men, but they found joy in killing nobles and this without hiding or during the night time."

"The people were so subjugated and frightened, but this did not keep them from boasting. They even had the audacity to choose among themselves pontiffs, not by lineage or nobility, but among their own partners in crime."

"They deceived anyone they could with words and fables, and not satisfied of persecuting men, they then decided to insult God by entering the forbidden place with dirty and damaged feet (The Holy place inside the Temple)."[38]

3. The Priests Ananus and Jeshua

At the time there were two righteous men who loved the city and its inhabitants and wanted to defend it from the havoc brought on by the Zealots. One of them was named Ananus (or Hanan), and the other was named Jeshua (not our Lord). They were loved by the people since they sought peace and treated everyone equal.

They knew the Romans could not be defeated and knew if the Jews did not learn to live peacefully, they would perish altogether.

---

[38] *The end of the paragraphs have been translated to modern english for better comprehension. War of the Jews page 378*

Ananus had been chosen to be the High priest and was considered the first and most wise among the Sadducees and Jeshua followed his position. Ananus led the people to rise up against the evil Zealots. The tyrants[39] had already taken the Temple and had made a fortress of the house of God to defend themselves against the people. It served as their habitation and meeting place.

In the midst of the tensions, the rest of the priests wanting to exert their authority, arrested Jacob, brother of the Lord Jesus Christ and several of his Christian partners. They formulated a false accusation against them as law breakers and were sentenced to death by stoning, near the Temple.[40]

Then they will deliver you up to tribulation and kill you, and you will be hated by all nations for My name's sake. And then many will be offended, will betray one another, and will hate one another. Then many false prophets will rise up and deceive many.

Matthew 24:9-11

"Another form of deceit was mixed in with all the evil and it would cause even more pain than everything done before. The tyrants decided to test the fear felt by the people as well as their strength by choosing the High Priest by the luck of the draw. They chose a rustic and rude man called Phannias. They dressed him with the clothing of the High Priest and

---

[39] *John of Gischala and the Zealots*

[40] *Josephus tells of the death of Jacob in "The Antiquities of the Jews 20:9"*

would tell him what to do. They considered this evil act to be a game and a joke."[41] "All of the other priests would look from afar and when they saw how they mocked the law, they could hardly hold back their tears and would cry out among each other at the sight of the honor of their priesthood and sacred items being ridiculed and mocked."[42]

"Unable to stand up to the affronts of the tyrants, Ananus and Jeshua organized the people to defeat the tyrants. Inconsolable, they would say: "Now if you have tyranny in so great a degree walled in, and see your enemies over your heads, to what purpose is it to take counsel? Perhaps you wait for the Romans, that they may protect our holy places: our matters then brought to that pass? And are we come to that degree of misery, that our enemies themselves are expected to pity us?"[43]

John, who was known for being deceitful, provoked the people against Ananus and Jeshua by spreading the rumor that Ananus wanted to give up the people to the Romans.

Many believed in this treachery, which falsely accused the pontiff, and decided to secretly send ambassadors with a letter to their neighbors to the south, the Idumeans. The letter asked the Idumeans to defend them against Ananus and the Romans.

---

[41] *Book IV chapter 3 page 206*

[42] *Book IV chapter 3 page 206*

[43] *Book IV chapter 3 page 207*

The Idumeans were ferocious and cruel Jews in war and men of great arrogance that deeply hated the Romans. When they read the demands in the letter, they became infuriated and armed themselves and declaring war. They recruited almost twenty thousand men with four captains and immediately arrived in Jerusalem.

Ananus and Jeshua, not knowing of the ambassadors, were surprised by the arrival of the armed Idumeans. However, being familiar with John and his tricks, they understood what they were doing there.

4. The Arrival of the Idumeans

Jeshua the Priest called out to them from one of the towers next to the wall saying, "For you have come to assist the vilest of men, and this with so great alacrity. These men who have invited you, every one of them would be found to have deserved ten thousand deaths; for the very rascality and off scouring of the whole country, who have spent in debauchery their own substance, and, by way of trial beforehand, have madly plundered the neighboring villages and cities, in the upshut of all, have privately run together into this holy city. They are robbers, who by their prodigious wickedness have profaned this most sacred floor, and who are to be now seen drinking themselves drunk in the sanctuary, and expending the spoils of those whom they have slaughtered upon their insatiable bellies. I cannot find good cause for why you have come against a group of people that have always been your friends, in favor of such thieves.[44]

---

[44] *Book IV chapter 4 page 212*

" You may, if you please, come into the city, though not in the way of war, and take a view of the marks still remaining of what I now say, and may see the houses that have been depopulated by their rapacious hands, with those wives and families that are in black, mourning for their slaughtered relations; as also you may hear the groans and lamentations all over the city; for there is nobody but had tasted of the incursions of these profane wretches, who have proceeded to that degree of madness that everything they have stolen from other cities as well as this one, the head of all Judea, has been taken to the Temple, the venerable place to the entire universe, honored by foreigners that came from all over the world just to see it. It is now stepped on and destroyed by the evil doers that have been born amongst us."[45]

Having said this and many other things, he tried to persuade them. They also closed the doors of the city so they would not enter.

Furious because they had rejected them and closed the city, the Idumeans decided to camp around the walls to defend the homeland and the Temple. Their exalted arrogance and bad temper would find no rest. They would not stand the insult thrown at them, and fearing the great strength of the Zealots, they regretted having gone.

They did not want to go back home, out of embarrassment. That is how twenty thousand men remained in the valley of Jehoshaphat next to the walls.

Having said these things, the Idumeans agreed to stay. Jeshua returned, saddened that they did not listen to reason or consent to something moderate.

[45] *Book IV chapter 4 page 213*

5. The Cold, The Storm and The Earthquake

"As they lay all night before the walls, though in a very bad encampment; for there broke out a prodigious storm in the night, with utmost violence, and very strong winds, with the largest showers of rain, with continued lightnings, terrible thunderings and amazing concussions and bellowings of the earth, that was in an earthquake. These things were a manifest indication that some destruction was coming upon men, when the system of the world was put into this disorder; and anyone would guess that these wonders foreshowed some grand calamities that were coming."[46]

"Now the opinion of the Idumeans and that of the city was one and the same. The Idumeans thought that God was angry at their taking arms and that they would not scape punishment for their making war against their metropolis."[47]

"Seeing the cold and the great storm intensifying, the Zealots decided to help the Idumeans since they believed it would be to their advantage to have so many people on their side. Even if helping them implied placing themselves in danger, they decided to do it anyway."

---

[46] *Book IV chapter 4 page 214*

[47] *Book IV chapter 4 page 215*

"Having taken advantage of the guards falling asleep due to the cold, as well as the loud sound caused by the storm and thunder, they secretly left the Temple and went to the wall of the city and made use of the saws of the Temple to open the door where the Idumeans were."

"At first there came a fear among the Idumeans themselves, which disturbed them as imagining that Ananus and his party were coming to attack them, so they took arms, but when they realized it was the Zealots, they went in little by little."

"Once they finally entered, the Zealots dared to all come out of the Temple and blended in with the Idumeans to come against the guards." "They killed some of the ones that had been sleeping, but the people woke up due to the screaming of the guards."

"The people thought the Zealots wanted to hurt them, but when they saw that the Idumeans had joined with them, they fainted."

"The young people in the city armed themselves and furiously rallied against them, resisting the attack. The screams of the people and the women were deafening and the Idumeans cried out as well. The storm caused the screams to be heard even louder. No one dared to assist another, they only returned the terrible echo of wailing and lamenting their misfortunes."

"The Idumeans forgave no one because they were cruel by nature in killing and the storm and the cold angered them. They considered those that had kept them outside of the city suffering, their enemies."

"Many who placed their relatives before them and begged them to have reverence towards the Temple, were killed. They had no way to escape and the assassins never backed down."[48]

"Due to the confusion and not knowing what they were doing, they killed each other with much more cruelty. So much so that the outer temple overflowing with blood; and that day, as it came on, they saw eight thousand five hundred men's dead bodies there."

"The rage of the Idumeans was not satisfied by these slaughters; but they now betook themselves to the city and plundered every house and slew everyone they met."

"Not satisfied with all the deaths, they sought to find the priests and High Priests and they placed all their effort into it. When they found them, they were cut them to pieces. They would stand on their bodies and mock and ridicule the friendship and love of Ananus towards the people and what Jeshua, the Priest had spoken to them from the wall."

"They showed their impious cruelty by throwing them out without a burial, knowing how important proper burials were to the Jews and how they would even bury the evildoers after sunset."[49]

---

[48] Book IV chapter 5 Page 216 extracts

[49] Book IV chapter 5 Page 216 extracts

6. The Death of Anano and Jeshua in the middle of the City

"I don't believe I would err in saying that Anano's death was the beginning of the destruction of the city and that the day the walls were destroyed so were the hearts of the people when they saw the pontiff and governor of everyone's well-being as well as Jeshua, higher than all the other priests, beheaded in the middle of the city."

"I cannot but think that God had doomed this city to destruction as a polluted city, and was resolved to purge His sanctuary by fire, that He cut off these their great defenders and well wishers, while those that a little before had worn the sacred garments, and had presided over the public worship… were cast out naked, and seem to be the food of dogs and wild beasts. I cannot but imagine that virtue itself groaned at these men's case, and lamented that she was here conquered by wickedness. And this at last was the end of Ananus and Jeshua."[50]

When I read this I could not stop thinking about the passage of the two witnesses. It could have been these two priests or not. Josephus generally testified from Titus' camp, outside of the city, so three days could have gone by without him testifying. There is no record of anyone writing from within the city, only Josephus, when he managed to enter.

Among so many deaths and hatred among one another, communication and writing was probably not very easy.

---

[50] *Book IV Chapter 5 page 217*

And their dead bodies will lie in the street of the great city which spiritually is called Sodom and Egypt, where also our Lord was crucified.

Then those from the peoples, tribes, tongues, and nations (The Jews of the nations who were trapped inside the city)[51] will see their dead bodies three-and-a-half days, and not allow their dead bodies to be put into graves.

And those who dwell on the earth will rejoice over them, make merry, and send gifts to one another, because these two prophets tormented those who dwell on the earth. (the territory)[52]

Now after the three-and-a-half days the breath of life from God entered them, and they stood on their feet, and great fear fell on those who saw them.

And they heard a loud voice from heaven saying to them, "Come up here." And they ascended to heaven in a cloud, and their enemies saw them. In the same hour there was a great earthquake, and a tenth of the city fell. In the earthquake seven thousand people were killed, and the rest were afraid and gave glory to the God of heaven.

Revelation 11:8-13

---

[51] *Parenthesis added to explain who they were.*

[52] *The word translated into English as earth is Ge in the Greek, which means territory or portion of a region. Strongs Concordance 1093: ge, portion of a territory.*

7. The Return of the Idumeans and the cruelty of the Zealots

"Now after these were slain (Ananus and Jeshua), the Zealots and the multitude of the Idumeans fell upon the people as upon a flock of profane animals, and cut their throats; wherever they were found, they would be killed."[53]

"The people were so terrified and in so much pain that none dared to cry in public or bury a single body no matter how close the relationship was. The prisoners would cry in secret fearing being heard by the guards. They would cry among each other and would secretly understand each other because if those that cried were heard, in that same moment they were punished and killed."

"Only in the night, they would take some dust and throw it upon their bodies; and even some that were the most ready to expose themselves to danger would do it in the day time: and there were twelve thousand of the better sort and noble men who perished in this manner."

"The Idumeans regretted going to Jerusalem and being deceived by the schemes of the Zealots."[54]

---

[53] *Book IV chapter 5 page 217*

[54] *Book IV chapter 5 page 217*

CHAPTER 8

THE HORRORS WITHIN THE CITY AND THE EXIT OF JESUS' DISCIPLES

1. The Gold that was stolen

"There were Syrians and Arabs in Jerusalem. They wanted to take the gold they had, and fearing the rebels would steal it, they would swallow it and remove it from their own excrement."

"Someone described this and it became well known throughout the camp that those that escaped were full of gold. So they threatened them saying they would open up their stomachs, but the covetousness was such that the Jews opened up the insides of two thousand men."[55]

"It was God who condemned the whole nation, and turned every course that was taken for their preservation to their destruction. These barbarians would go out, and meet those that ran away before anyone saw them, and looking about them to see that no Roman spied them, they dissected them and pulled this polluted money out of their bowels which money was still found in few of them, while yet a great many were destroyed by the bare hope there was of thus getting by them."[56]

---

[55] *Extracts and summary Book V, Chapter 13 page 287 -288*

[56] *Extracts and summary Book V, Chapter 13 page-288*

2. The Sacrilege committed in The Temple and the number of dead in the City

"With nothing left to take in the city, John committed a sacrilege and began to sack the Temple and robbed many things and consecrated vessels used for divine service."

"The Roman Emperors had always honored the Temple and had gifted many ornaments for it."

"Then a Jew (among the Zealots) that sacked and destroyed the Temple would tell his partners, without fear, that they should make use of the sacred things and that those who fought for the honor of God and the temple should be fed and sustained by the riches of the temple.

They figured it was a licit thing to pour out the oil that the priests stored for their sacrifices and drink the sacred wine. He then distributed this among the people and they anointed themselves with oil and drank without apprehension."[57]

The grain offering and the drink offering have been cut off from the house of the Lord; the priests mourn, who minister to the Lord. The field is wasted, the land mourns; for the grain is ruined, the new wine is dried up, the oil fails.

---

[57] *Extracts and summary Book V, Chapter 13 page 288*

Consecrate a fast, call a sacred assembly; gather the elders and all the inhabitants of the land[58] into the house of the Lord your God, and cry out to the Lord. Alas for the day! For the day of the Lord is at hand; it shall come as destruction from the Almighty.

Joel 1: 9-10 & 14-15

3. God gives his believers a way out

There were two clear occasions, according to history in which God gave the new Church the opportunity to escape just as Jesus had predicted to His disciples.

The first one was during the first siege in Jerusalem in November of 66 A.D., led by the Roman General Cestius.[59]

He had been sent by Nero to appease the first revolts that broke out in Caesarea, but he had also been instructed to take all of Judea. He attacked several cities, interrupted the Feast of the Tabernacles and while setting fire to the suburbs, he entered Jerusalem.

He took the high city and camped out in front of the royal palace. At the time, many of Jesus' disciples were trapped by the siege in the zone of the Temple, being surrounded by Romans that were stationed next to the walls.

---

[58] *"Inhabitants of the land" does not refer to the entire world. It refers to the territory of Israel. Obviously, the entire world does not fit inside a Temple.*

[59] *Cestius Gallus fell in 67 A.D. He was the son of a counsel in Ancient Rome and he was counsel suffectus himself in 42 A.D. He was a representative in Syria in 63 A.D. or 65 A.D. He marched to Judea in 66 A.D. in an attempt to restore peace at the beginning of the Great Jewish Rebellion.*

The providence of God intervened then. Josephus says of Cestius:

"Had Cestius forced the entry into the fortresses, the city would have fallen and the war would have ended, but the prefect of the camp, the tyrant Prisco, was bribed to prolong the war by Gessius Florus, (District Attorney in Judea) and he diverted the attempt."[60]

"If he had only persisted in continuing the siege, he would have taken the city, but be it as it may Cestius suddenly called back his troops and left the city with no justification."

"The disciples that were more alert took advantage of this withdrawal to leave the city and found refuge in Mount Pella."[61]

The second opportunity came two years later in 68 A.D.. Rome had returned to surround Jerusalem and General Vespasian abandoned the siege to attend the Emperor Nero's funeral in Alexandria. This is the other sign, the Christians who were filled with the Holy Spirit took advantage of, to flee from the city. They knew the Romans would return at any moment, so obeying the instructions of their Teacher, they fled to the mountains. Many other Jewish people who had accepted Jesus as the Messiah, had grown cold and missed the opportunity to escape.

---

[60] *Book II, Chapter 19, extracts from Pages 145-147*

[61] *Christian Mount Sion Franciscan Cyberspot*

http://www.christuxres.org/www1/ofm/san/TSsion001_ES.html

Therefore when you see the 'abomination of desolation,' spoken of by Daniel the prophet, standing in the holy place" (whoever reads, let him understand), "then let those who are in Judea flee to the mountains. Let him who is on the housetop not go down to take anything out of his house. And let him who is in the field not go back to get his clothes.

Matthew 24:15-18

The abomination of desolation referred to all the horrors and sacrileges that were committed inside the temple. Aside from this, the Romans had hung and imperial eagle in the main door of the Temple.[62]

The Israel that was filled with the Spirit of God was protected by their Lord, but the lukewarm and idle died in the siege.

The doors to escape had been closed and only a horrible expectation of the Judgment was left.

Jesus, referring to Israel, who His ministry was devoted to, made an analogy of the ten virgins. Five of them were prudent and the others were not.

Jesus was the Son of God that came to unite His spirit with His bride. This bride was first and foremost Jewish, and would enjoy salvation with the foreign believers (inside the city) as well as God's protection during the siege.

---

[62] *Book I, Chapter 33, Page 90*

And while they went to buy, the bridegroom came, and those who were ready went in with him to the wedding; and the door was shut. Afterward the other virgins came also, saying, 'Lord, Lord, open to us!'

But he answered and said, 'Assuredly, I say to you, I do not know you.'

"Watch therefore, for you know neither the day nor the hour in which the Son of Man is coming.

Matthew 25:10-13

This prophecy is directly related to the judgment that would come in 70 A.D. Jesus warns them that not everyone would be ready and the judgment that would suddenly come, required that they be attentive to the Holy Spirit. (Lamps full of oil)

From the end of Matthew chapter 23 to the end of chapter 25, Jesus is speaking of the destruction of Jerusalem and the judgment that would bring the end. He is not speaking of the marriage blessing in itself, but of the importance of being prepared.

This parable is parallel to the passage in Revelation 19 where we see the spiritual union of Jesus with His people as a wedding. This takes place by being filled with the Spirit of God and participating in the Lord's Supper. After this union, Jesus comes with His armies and His saints to step on the wine of the evil of Jerusalem and put an end to the Mosaic age.

Then he said to me, "Write: 'Blessed are those who are called to the marriage supper of the Lamb!'" And he said to me, "These are the true sayings of God."

*Now I saw heaven opened, and behold, a white horse. And He who sat on him was called Faithful and True, and in righteousness He judges and makes war. His eyes were like a flame of fire, and on His head were many crowns. **He had a name written that no one knew except Himself.***

He was clothed with a robe dipped in blood, and His name is called THE WORD OF GOD. And the armies in heaven, clothed in fine linen, white and clean, followed Him on white horses.

*Now out of His mouth goes a sharp sword, that with it He should strike the nations. And He Himself will rule them with a rod of iron. He Himself treads the winepress of the fierceness and wrath of Almighty God. And He has on His robe and on His thigh a name written: **KING OF KINGS AND LORD OF LORDS.***

Revelation 19:9 & 11-16

Note that the title of King of Kings and Lord of Lords is linked to the Marriage Supper of the Lamb and His Coming on a Horse to bring the judgment upon His vineyard . If this word were for the future, as it is believed traditionally, then this suggests that Jesus is not King of Kings or Lord of Lords yet. He descended with His armies in His majestic presence (parousia) during the judgment of 70 A.D., as we will see later.

95

I will speak in more detail regarding the meaning of the Wedding of the Lamb in the Question Section of this book.

4. The Army of Simon Bar Giora

After Nero's death in 68 A.D. there was a great amount of instability in Rome. Four emperors came about during the following year, so the wall surrounding Jerusalem was less protected.

The Jewish did not take advantage of this time to be strengthened, but on the contrary, they fought among themselves.

While John and the Zealots occupied the Temple in Jerusalem, there arose another war in Jerusalem.

"There was a son of Giora, one Simon, by birth of Gerasa, a young man, not so cunning indeed as John [of Gisehala], who had already seized upon the city, but superior in strength of body and courage; on which account, when he had been driven away from that Acrabatene toparchy, which he once had, by Ananus the high priest, he came to those robbers who had seized upon Masada. At the first they suspected him, and only permitted him to come with the women he brought with him into the lower part of the fortress, while they dwelt in the upper part of it themselves. However, his manner so well agreed with theirs, and he seemed so trusty a man, that he went out with them, and ravaged and destroyed the country with them about Masada; yet when he persuaded them to undertake greater things, he could not prevail with them so to do; for as they were accustomed to dwell in that citadel, they were afraid of going far from that which was their hiding-place; but he affecting to tyrannize, and being fond of greatness, when he had heard of the death of Ananus, he left them, and went into the mountainous part of the country. So he proclaimed liberty to those in slavery, and a reward to those already free, and got together a set of wicked men from all quarters."

"And as he had now a strong body of men about him, he overran the villages that lay in the mountainous country, and when there were still more and more that came to him, he ventured to go down into the lower parts of the country, and since he was now become formidable to the cities, many of the men of power were corrupted by him; so that his army was no longer composed of slaves and robbers, but a great many of the populace were obedient to him as to their king. He then overran the Acrabattene toparchy, and the places that reached as far as the Great Idumea; for he built a wall at a certain village called Nain, and made use of that as a fortress for his own party's security; and at the valley called Paran, he enlarged many of the caves, and many others he found ready for his purpose; these he made use of as repositories for his treasures, and receptacles for his prey, and therein he laid up the fruits that he had got by rapine; and many of his partisans had their dwelling in them; and he made no secret of it that he was exercising his men beforehand, and making preparations for the assault of Jerusalem."

"Whereupon the zealots, out of the dread they were in of his attacking them, and being willing to prevent one that was growing up to oppose them, went out against him with their weapons. Simon met them, and joining battle with them, slew a considerable number of them, and drove the rest before him into the city, but durst not trust so much upon his forces as to make an assault upon the walls; but he resolved first to subdue Idumea, and as he had now twenty thousand armed men, he marched to the borders of their country."[63]

"Simon then entered into the remaining parts of Idumea plundering and destroying the ground; cutting down trees and destroying the fields. They became as hardened as the most infertile ground in the world; so much so that there was absolutely no sign that anything had ever been there even when they walked on the ground."[64]

Prophet Joel spoke of this devastating army that would rise in the midst of the darkest and most dramatic days in Israel.

This could have well been both Simon and John's armies.

A day of darkness and gloominess, a day of clouds and thick darkness, like the morning clouds spread over the mountains. A people come, great and strong, the like of whom has never been; nor will there ever be any such after them, even for many successive generations.

*A fire devours before them, and behind them a flame burns; the land is like the Garden of Eden before them, and **behind them a desolate wilderness**; surely nothing shall escape them.*

---

[63] *Book IV Chapter 9 page 231*

[64] *Book IV Chapter 9 page 232 Extract*

Their appearance is like the appearance of horses;
and like swift steeds, so they run.

With a noise like chariots over mountaintops they
leap, like the noise of a flaming fire that devours the
stubble, like a strong people set in battle array.

They run to and fro in the city, they run on the wall;
they climb into the houses, they enter at the windows
like a thief.

The earth quakes before them, the heavens tremble;
the sun and moon grow dark, and the stars diminish
their brightness.

Joel 2:2-5 & 9-10

After this encounter, the Zealots decided to send spies and guards to Simon's camp hoping to kidnap his wife. They believed this would cause him to stop and ask them for peace.

"This success of Simon excited the zealots afresh; and though they were afraid to fight him openly in a fair battle, yet did they lay ambushes in the passes, and seized upon his wife, with a considerable number of her attendants; whereupon they came back to the city rejoicing, as if they had taken Simon himself captive, and were in present expectation that he would lay down his arms, and make supplication to them for his wife; but instead of indulging any merciful affection, he grew very angry at them for seizing his beloved wife; so he came to the wall of Jerusalem, and, like wild beasts when they are wounded, and cannot overtake those that wounded them, he vented his spleen upon all persons that he met with. Accordingly, he caught all those that were come out of the city gates, either to gather herbs or sticks, who were unarmed and in years; he then tormented them and destroyed them, out of the immense rage he was in, and was almost ready to taste the very flesh of their dead bodies. He also cut off the hands of a great many, and sent them into the city to astonish his enemies, and in order to make the people fall into a sedition, and desert those that had been the authors of his wife's seizure. He also enjoined them to tell the people that Simon swore by the God of the universe, who sees all things, that unless they will restore him his wife, he will break down their wall, and inflict the like punishment upon all the citizens, without sparing any age, and without making any distinction between the guilty and the innocent. These threatenings so greatly affrighted, not the people only, but the zealots themselves also, that they sent his wife back to him; when he became a little milder, and left off his perpetual blood-shedding."[65]

5. The Number of Dead in The Valley of Decision

Within the city, things were going from bad to worse. The deaths of Ananus and Jeshua added to the desire John and the Zealots' had to impose their terror on the people, brought great internal destruction.

For days will come upon you when your enemies will build an embankment around you, surround you and close you in on every side, and level you, and your children within you, to the ground;

---

[65] *Book IV Chapter 9 page 232 and 233*

*and they will not leave in you one stone upon
another, because you did not know the time of your
visitation.*

Luke 19:43-44

Flavius adds:

"I will not stop saying what pain forces me to say. I believe
that if the Romans stopped for a moment and tarried in
coming against those evil people, or if the earth opened and
swallowed up the city, or it perished due to a flood or if it was
consumed by the fire of Sodom because these people were
worse and much more impious than those people."

"And, indeed, why do I relate these particular calamities?
While Manneus, the son of Lazarus, came running to Titus
at this very time, and told him that there had been carried
out through that one gate, which was intrusted to his care,
no fewer than a hundred and fifteen thousand eight hundred
and eighty dead bodies, in the interval between the fourteenth
day of the month Xanthieus, [Nisan,] when the Romans
pitched their camp by the city, and the first day of the month
Panemus [Tamuz]. This was itself a prodigious multitude;
and though this man was not himself set as a governor at that
gate, yet was he appointed to pay the public stipend for
carrying these bodies out, and so was obliged of necessity to
number them, while the rest were buried by their relations;
though all their burial was but this, to bring them away, and
cast them out of the city."

"After this man there ran away to Titus many of the eminent
citizens, and told him the entire number of the poor that were
dead, and that no fewer than six hundred thousand were

thrown out at the gates, though still the number of the rest could not be discovered; and they told him further, that when they were no longer able to carry out the dead bodies of the poor, they laid their corpses on heaps in very large houses, and shut them up therein."[66]

"As also that a half of a measure of wheat was sold for a talent; and that when, a while afterward, it was not possible to gather herbs, by reason the city was all walled about, some persons were driven to that terrible distress as to search the common sewers and old dunghills of cattle, and to eat the dung which they got there; and what they of old could not endure so much as to see they now used for food."[67]

And the songs of the temple shall be wailing in that day," says the Lord God—"Many dead bodies everywhere, they shall be thrown out in silence."

Amos 8:3

The dead were mainly thrown in the Valley of Jehoshaphat or the Valley of Decision, since it was the closest to the Temple and the place where the most intense revolts and crimes took place.

We will see towards the end of the destruction of Jerusalem how this valley fills up with dead bodies and how the Roman armies rode their horses on the dead.

According to Josephus, over 600,000 men were thrown in there.

---

[66] *Book V Chapter 13 page 288*

[67] *Book V Chapter 13 page 288*

And the winepress was trampled outside the city, and blood came out of the winepress, up to the horses' bridles, for one thousand six hundred furlongs.

Revelation 14:20

Valley of Jehoshaphat

Temple

Roman Walls During The Siege

Fig. 5 — Siege of The Walls of Jerusalem

Let the nations be wakened, and come up to the Valley of Jehoshaphat; for there I will sit to judge all the surrounding nations.

Put in the sickle, for the harvest is ripe. Come, go down; for the winepress is full, the vats overflow — for their wickedness is great."

Multitudes, multitudes in the valley of decision! For the day of the Lord is near in the valley of decision.

Joel 3:12-14

When the Son of Man comes in His glory, and all the holy angels with Him, then He will sit on the throne of His glory. All the nations will be gathered before Him, and He will separate them one from another, as a shepherd divides his sheep from the goats.

Matthew 25:31-32

All of these scriptures are related to this judgment in the Jewish nations as well as the nations that made up the Roman Empire. Jesus came to execute this judgment with His Radiant Light (*Epifania*) which radiated from heaven to bring an end to that era of evil, corruption and apostasy.

We must remember that Jesus' ministry in the flesh was for the Jews and that He came to fulfill what was written, including the day of the vengeance of The Living God.

Flavius Josephus continues:

"by this reason the city was all walled about, some persons were driven to that terrible distress as to search the common sewers and old dunghills of cattle, and to eat the dung which they got there; and what they of old could not endure so much as to see they now used for food. When the Romans barely heard all this, they commiserated their case; while the seditious, who saw it also, did not repent, but suffered the same distress to come upon themselves; for they were blinded by that fate which was already coming upon the city, and upon themselves also."[68]

THUS did the miseries of Jerusalem grow worse and worse every day, and the seditious were still more irritated by the calamities they were under, even while the famine preyed upon themselves, after it had preyed upon the people. And indeed the multitude of carcasses that lay in heaps one upon another was a horrible sight, and produced a pestilential stench, which was a hinderance to those that would make sallies out of the city, and fight the enemy: but as those were to go in battle-array, who had been already used to ten thousand murders, and must tread upon those dead bodies as they marched along, so were not they terrified, nor did they pity men as they marched over them; nor did they deem this affront offered to the deceased to be any ill omen to themselves; but as they had their right hands already polluted with the murders of their own countrymen, and in that condition ran out to fight with foreigners, they seem to me to have cast a reproach upon God himself, as if he were too

[68] *Book V Chapter 13 page 289*

slow in punishing them; for the war was not now gone on with as if they had any hope of victory; for they gloried after a brutish manner in that despair of deliverance they were already in."

" And now the Romans, although they were greatly distressed in getting together their materials, raised their banks in one and twenty days, after they had cut down all the trees that were in the country that adjoined to the city, and that for ninety furlongs[69] round about, as I have already related. And truly the very view itself of the country was a melancholy thing; for those places which were before adorned with trees and pleasant gardens were now become a desolate country every way, and its trees were all cut down: nor could any foreigner that had formerly seen Judea and the most beautiful suburbs of the city, and now saw it as a desert."[70]

> *The field is wasted, the land mourns; for the grain is ruined, the new wine is dried up, the oil fails.*
>
> *Be ashamed, you farmers, wail, you vinedressers, for the wheat and the barley; because the harvest of the field has perished.*
>
> *Is not the food cut off before our eyes, joy and gladness from the house of our God?*
>
> *How the animals groan! The herds of cattle are restless, because they have no pasture; even the flocks of sheep suffer punishment.*
>
> *Joel 1:10-11 & 16-18*

---

[69] *aproximately 20 miles (abt. 32 kilometers).*

[70] *Book VI Chapter 1 Page 291*

Seeing so much internal destruction, Josephus decided to attempt to persuade John and his compatriots to cease the internal fight. He cried out to them:

"And who is there that does not know what the writings of the ancient prophets contain in them, - and particularly that oracle which is just now going to be fulfilled upon this miserable city? For they foretold that this city should be then taken when somebody shall begin the slaughter of his own countrymen. And are not both the city and the entire temple now full of the dead bodies of your countrymen? It is God, therefore, it is God himself who is bringing on this fire, to purge that city and temple by means of the Romans, and is going to pluck up this city, which is full of your pollutions."[71]

"As Josephus spoke these words, with groans and tears in his eyes, his voice was intercepted by sobs. However, the Romans could not but pity the affliction he was under, and wonder at his conduct."[72]

John ignored the words of Josephus, but the nobles and many of the priests reasoned, considered their own well being and decided to flee. They made a covenant of protection with the Romans who even promised to return their belongings.

That is why only those who became Roman allies had the opportunity to survive. The war, the gate, the hunger and the robberies had become intolerable. There was no commerce or supplies, only great suffering and the pestilence of the dead in the city. That is why only those who joined with the Romans had access to buy and sell.

---

[71] *Book VI Chapter 2 Page 298*

[72] *Book VI Chapter 2 Page 298*

... and that no one may buy or sell except one who has the mark or the name of the beast, or the number of his name.

Revelation 13:17

When John's people saw the exodus of those who became Roman allies, they made a huge ruckus promulgating that the Romans had killed those who had joined with them. That is how they prevented the poor and those who were still with them to flee as well. But the Romans, who did not want the Temple to be destroyed by John because they truly valued it, had the nobles show themselves above the gate so the others could see they were alive.

This exposed the tyrant and his lies which he used to control the Jews. Many abandoned him and joined in with the Romans.

Titus would let many of them go through the camps wherever they wished and this caused many others to want to flee because they saw those who fled as being free from all the damage they suffered inside. They also wanted to be free from Roman servant hood.

John and Simon, along with their people, worked to not only close the exit, but also the entrance of the Romans. Those who would try to leave were killed. The rich who died would not only die from fleeing, but by staying. They were killed for the same cause-to take their riches.

CHAPTER 9

THE GREAT FAMINE PRODUCED BY THE SIEGE OF THE CITY AND THOSE CRUCIFIED ON THE WALLS

"Now of those that perished by famine in the city, the number was prodigious, and the miseries they underwent were unspeakable. If the shadow of any kind of food did any where appear, a war was commenced presently, and the dearest friends fought one with another about it, snatching from each other the most miserable supports of life. Nor would men believe that those who were dying had no food, but the robbers would search them when they were expiring, lest any one should have concealed food in their bosoms, and counterfeited dying; nay, these robbers gaped for want, and ran about stumbling and staggering along like mad dogs, and reeling against the doors of the houses like drunken men; they would also, in the great distress they were in, rush into the very same houses two or three times in one and the same day.

Moreover, their hunger was so intolerable, that it obliged them to chew every thing, while they gathered such things as the most sordid animals would not touch, and endured to eat them; nor did they at length abstain from girdles and shoes; and the very leather which belonged to their shields they pulled off and gnawed: the very wisps of old hay became food to some; **and some gathered up grain, and sold a very small**

109

weight of them for four Attic [drachmae]. But why do I describe the shameless impudence that the famine brought on men in their eating inanimate things, while I am going to relate a matter of fact, the like to which no history relates, either among the Greeks or Barbarians? It is horrible to speak of it, and incredible when heard. I had indeed willingly omitted this calamity of ours ..."[73]

"As also that a half of a measure of wheat was sold for a talent; and that when, a while afterward, it was not possible to gather herbs, because the city was all walled about, some persons were driven to that terrible distress as to search the common sewers and old dunghills of cattle, and to eat the dung which they got there"[74]

> *When He opened the third seal, I heard the third living creature say, "Come and see." So I looked, and behold, a black horse, and he who sat on it had a pair of scales in his hand. And I heard a voice in the midst of the four living creatures saying, "A quart of wheat for a denarius, and three quarts of barley for a denarius; and do not harm the oil and the wine."*
>
> *Revelation 6:5-6*

"It was now a miserable case, and a sight that would justly bring tears into our eyes, how men stood as to their food, while the more powerful had more than enough, and the weaker were lamenting [for want of it.]

---

[73] *Book VI Chapter 3 page 304*

[74] *Book V Chapter 13 page 288*

But the famine was too hard for all other passions, and it is destructive to nothing so much as to modesty; for what was otherwise worthy of reverence was in this case despised; insomuch that children pulled the very morsels that their fathers were eating out of their very mouths, and what was still more to be pitied, so did the mothers do as to their infants; and when those that were most dear were perishing under their hands, they were not ashamed to take from them the very last drops that might preserve their lives: and while they ate after this manner, yet were they not concealed in so doing; but the seditious every where came upon them immediately, and snatched away from them what they had gotten from others; for when they saw any house shut up, this was to them a signal that the people within had gotten some food; whereupon they broke open the doors, and ran in, and took pieces of what they were eating almost up out of their very throats, and this by force.

The old men, who held their food fast, were beaten; and if the women hid what they had within their hands, their hair was torn for so doing; nor was there any commiseration shown either to the aged or to the infants, but they lifted up children from the ground as they hung upon the morsels they had gotten, and shook them down upon the floor.

But still they were more barbarously cruel to those that had prevented their coming in, and had actually swallowed down what they were going to seize upon, as if they had been unjustly defrauded of their right. They also invented terrible methods of torments to discover where any food was, and they were these to stop up the passages of the privy parts of the miserable wretches, and to drive sharp stakes up their fundaments.

And a man was forced to bear what it is terrible even to hear, in order to make him confess that he had but one loaf of bread, or that he might discover a handful of barley-meal that was concealed; and this was done when these tormentors were not themselves hungry; for the thing had been less barbarous had necessity forced them to it; but this was done to keep their madness in exercise, and as making preparation of provisions for themselves for the following days.

These men went also to meet those that had crept out of the city by night, as far as the Roman guards, to gather some plants and herbs that grew wild; and when those people thought they had got clear of the enemy, they snatched from them what they had brought with them, even while they had frequently entreated them, and that by calling upon the tremendous name of God, to give them back some part of what they had brought; though these would not give them the least crumb, and they were to be well contented that they were only spoiled, and not slain at the same time.

These were the afflictions which the lower sort of people suffered from these tyrants' guards; but for the men that were in dignity, and withal were rich, they were carried before the tyrants themselves; some of whom were falsely accused of laying treacherous plots, and so were destroyed; others of them were charged with designs of betraying the city to the Romans; but the readiest way of all was this, to suborn somebody to affirm that they were resolved to desert to the enemy. And he who was utterly despoiled of what he had by Simon was sent back again to John, as of those who had been already plundered by Simon got what remained; insomuch that they drank the blood of the populace to one another, and divided the dead bodies of the poor creatures between them;

so that although, on account of their ambition after dominion, they contended with each other, yet did they very well agree in their wicked practices; for he that did not communicate what he got by the miseries of others to the other tyrant seemed to be too little guilty, and in one respect only;

It is therefore impossible to go distinctly over every instance of these men's iniquity. I shall therefore speak my mind here at once briefly: - That neither did any other city ever suffer such miseries, nor did any age ever breed a generation more fruitful in wickedness than this was, from the beginning of the world."[75]

"The Jews were stripped of their right and ability to leave and that is how they lost all hope to be saved. Hunger had already entered all the homes and all the families. The homes were filled with women and children who died of starvation and the streets were lined with dead old men. Young people and children were seen in the market place and market square and they had no color to them as if dead already. When someone would die everyone became frightened because they had no way to bury the dead due to the amount of work this implied. Those that had little strength left would shy away and would not do it in part because they would see the great number of people and in part because they knew the end that was awaiting them as well."

"Many would end up dying on top of those they did bury. Many would run off and bury themselves alive before their own end came. Their crying and moaning was not heard because the starvation they suffered would not allow it.

---

[75] *Book V Chapter 10 pages 277 and 278*

The last to die would look up on the first to die and could see their dry eyes, so lifeless that they were unable to produce a single tear. Their mouths and stomachs were corrupted."

The city was silent, full of darkness and death. The thieves caused even more bitterness and crying than everything else. They would empty the homes, which were nothing more than tombs for the dead. They would strip the clothing from the dead and would come out laughing and mocking. They would test their swords on them and in doing so, would end up killing some that were still alive. When one of them begged them for help or asked them to kill them in order to be free from the dangers of hunger, they were scorned in an arrogant way."

Judas (Thaddeus) and Enoch wrote of this:

"...raging waves of the sea, foaming up their own shame; wandering stars for whom is reserved the blackness of darkness forever.

Now Enoch, the seventh from Adam, prophesied about these men also, saying, "Behold, the Lord comes with ten thousands of His saints, to execute judgment on all, to convict all who are ungodly among them of all their ungodly deeds which they have committed in an ungodly way, and of all the harsh things which ungodly sinners have spoken against Him."

Jude 13-15

"Those who died would turn their eyes toward the Temple and felt much sorrow that only the rebels were kept alive."

"At first they used public money to bury the dead, unable to stand the horrible stench, but it was not enough. They ended up throwing them out from the wall and unto the valleys and trenches."

"Upon hearing of this, the Romans felt mercy, but the wicked and seditious rebels did not repent upon seeing this, they simply tolerated them."

The Account of when they ate their Children due to Hunger

I will make this city desolate and a hissing; everyone who passes by it will be astonished and hiss because of all its plagues. And I will cause them to eat the flesh of their sons and the flesh of their daughters, and everyone shall eat the flesh of his friend in the siege and in the desperation with which their enemies and those who seek their lives shall drive them to despair.

Jeremiah 19:8-9

This prophecy was fulfilled during the first destruction of Jerusalem by Nebuchadnezzar, King of Babylon, but it also echoes during the final destruction of the holy city.

Josephus wrote about this terrible event:

"A woman named Mary, rich and of noble lineage had fled away to Jerusalem with the rest of the multitude, and was with them besieged therein at this time. All of her belongings were stolen by tyrants."[76]

"…And it was now become impossible for her any way to find any more food, while the famine pierced through her very bowels and marrow, when also her passion was fired to a degree beyond the famine itself; nor did she consult with anything but with her passion and the necessity she was in. She then attempted a most unnatural thing; and snatching up her son, who was a child sucking at her breast, she said, "O thou miserable infant! for whom shall I preserve thee in this war, this famine, and this sedition? As to the war with the Romans, if they preserve our lives, we must be slaves. This famine also will destroy us, even before that slavery comes upon us. Yet are these seditious rogues more terrible than both the other. Come on; be thou my food, and be thou a fury to these seditious varlets, and a by-word to the world, which is all that is now wanting to complete the calamities of us Jews." As soon as she had said this, she slew her son, and then roasted him, and eat the one half of him, and kept the other half by her concealed. Upon this the seditious came in presently, and smelling the horrid scent of this food, they threatened her that they would cut her throat immediately if she did not show them what food she had gotten ready. She replied that she had saved a very fine portion of it for them, and withal uncovered what was left of her son.

Hereupon they were seized with a horror and amazement of mind, and stood astonished at the sight, when she said to them, "This is mine own son, and what hath been done was mine own doing! Come, eat of this food; for I have eaten of it myself!"[77]

Fig. 6 — Mary, who killed her child to eat him

The city was then filled with this evil act."

"This sad instance was quickly told to the Romans, some of whom could not believe it, and others pitied the distress which the Jews were under; but there were many of them who were hereby induced to a more bitter hatred than ordinary against our nation."

---

[77] *Book VI Chapter 3, page 304-305*

"But for Caesar, he excused himself before God as to this matter, and said that he had proposed peace and liberty to the Jews, as well as an oblivion of all their former insolent practices; but that they, instead of concord, had chosen sedition; instead of peace, war; and before satiety and abundance, a famine. That they had begun with their own hands to burn down that temple which we have preserved hitherto; and that therefore they deserved to eat such food as this was. That, however, this horrid action of eating an own child ought to be covered with the overthrow of their very country itself, and men ought not to leave such a city upon the habitable earth to be seen by the sun, wherein mothers are thus fed, although such food be fitter for the fathers than for the mothers to eat of, since it is they that continue still in a state of war against us, after they have undergone such miseries as these." [78]

Jesus also prophesied about this when He spoke to the women of Jerusalem:

But Jesus, turning to them, said, "Daughters of Jerusalem, do not weep for Me, but weep for yourselves and for your children. For indeed the days are coming in which they will say, 'Blessed are the barren, wombs that never bore, and breasts which never nursed!' Then they will begin 'to say to the mountains, "Fall on us!" and to the hills, "Cover us!"

Luke 23:28-30

---

[78] *Book VI Chapter 3, page 305*

The Account of the Jews who were crucified on the wall

"So now Titus's banks were advanced a great way, notwithstanding his soldiers had been very much distressed from the wall. He then sent a party of horsemen, and ordered they should lay ambushes for those that went out into the valleys to gather food. Some of these were indeed fighting men, who were not contented with what they got by rapine; but the greater part of them were poor people, who were deterred from deserting by the concern they were under for their own relations; for they could not hope to escape away, together with their wives and children, without the knowledge of the seditious; nor could they think of leaving these relations to be slain by the robbers on their account;"

"they were forced to defend themselves for fear of being punished; as after they had fought, they thought it too late to make any supplications for mercy; so they were first whipped, and then tormented with all sorts of tortures, before they died, and were then crucified before the wall of the city. This miserable procedure made Titus greatly to pity them, while they caught every day five hundred Jews; nay, some days they caught more."

"So the soldiers, out of the wrath and hatred they bore the Jews, nailed those they caught, one after one way, and another after another, to the crosses, by way of jest, when their multitude was so great, that room was wanting for the crosses, and crosses wanting for the bodies."[79]

---

[79] *Book V Chapter 11, page 279*

"yet did some of them run away immediately as unto certain punishment, esteeming death from their enemies to be a quiet departure, if compared with that by famine. So Titus commanded that the hands of many of those that were caught should be cut off, that they might not be thought deserters, and might be credited on account of the calamity they were under, and sent them in to John and Simon, with this exhortation, that they would now at length leave off [their madness], and not force him to destroy the city, whereby they would have those advantages of repentance, even in their utmost distress, that they would preserve their own lives, and so find a city of their own."[80]

Some were put in prison and crucified and others were set free.

Then two men will be in the field: one will be taken and the other left. Two women will be grinding at the mill: one will be taken and the other left.

Matthew 24:40-41

When Jesus prophesied regarding those who would be taken, He was referring to the prophecy declared by Prophet Zechariah:

Behold, the day of the Lord is coming, and your spoil will be divided in your midst.

---

[80] *Book V Chapter 11, page 279*

For I will gather all the nations[81] to battle against Jerusalem; The city shall be taken, the houses rifled, and the women ravished.

Half of the city shall go into captivity, but the remnant of the people shall not be cut off from the city.

Zechariah 14:1-2

*Fig. 7 — Those crucified by Titus
outside of the walls of Jerusalem*

---

[81] *Group of nations that formed the Roman Empire, which was the ruling territory of the world at the time.*

CHAPTER 10

THE DESTRUCTION OF THE TEMPLE

*Then Jesus went out and departed from the temple,
and His disciples came up to show Him the buildings
of the temple. And Jesus said to them, "Do you not
see all these things? Assuredly, I say to you, not one
stone shall be left here upon another, that shall not
be thrown down.*

Matthew 24:1-2

Flavius Josephus tries to convince the Jews to surrender

"Upon this Josephus stood in such a place where he might be heard, not by John only, but by many more, and then declared to them what Caesar had given him in charge, and this in the Hebrew language. So he earnestly prayed them to spare their own city, and to prevent that fire which was just ready to seize upon the temple, and to offer their usual sacrifices to God therein. At these words of his a great sadness and silence were observed among the people. But the tyrant himself cast many reproaches upon Josephus, with imprecations besides; and at last added this withal, that he did never fear the taking of the city, because it was God's own city. In answer to which Josephus said thus with a loud voice: "To be sure you have kept this city wonderfully pure for

123

God's sake; the temple also continues entirely unpolluted! Nor have you been guilty of ally impiety against him for whose assistance thou hoped! He still receives his accustomed sacrifices! Vile wretch that you are! If any one should deprive thee of thy daily food, thou wouldst esteem him to be an enemy to thee; but you hoped to have that God for thy supporter in this war whom you had deprived of his everlasting worship; and you imputed those sins to the Romans, who to this very time take care to have our laws observed, and almost compel these sacrifices to be still offered to God"[82]

Josephus continued speaking, not wanting to see the city submerged in such a horrendous ending and he would say to them:

"And who is there that does not know what the writings of the ancient prophets contain in them, - and particularly that oracle which is just now going to be fulfilled upon this miserable city? For they foretold that this city should be then taken when somebody shall begin the slaughter of his own countrymen. And are not both the city and the entire temple now full of the dead bodies of your countrymen? It is God, therefore, it is God himself who is bringing on this fire, to purge that city and temple by means of the Romans, and is going to pluck up this city, which is full of your pollutions."[83]

Upon hearing this, John and his partners came against the Romans even stronger.

---

[82] *Book VI Chapter 2 page 297*

[83] *Book VI Chapter 2 page 297*

"Many also of the other nobility went over to the Romans, together with the high priests. Now Caesar not only received these men very kindly in other respects, but, knowing they would not willingly live after the customs of other nations, he sent them to Gophna, and desired them to remain there for the present, and told them, that when he was gotten clear of this war, he would restore each of them to their possessions again; so they cheerfully retired to that small city which was allotted them, without fear of any danger."[84]

They could now buy and sell and be protected, having made an allegiance with Rome.

And he causeth all, both small and great, rich and poor, free and bond, to receive a mark in their right hand, or in their foreheads:

And that no man might buy or sell, save he that had the mark, or the name of the beast, or the number of his name.

Revelation 13:16-17

The Account on How The Exterior Wall of The Temple Was Brought Down and The Beginning of The Fire

Around the 8th day of August (70 A.D.), General Titus ordered his troops to go to the exterior part of the Temple on the west side, with their inventiveness and their machines.

Six days before that he had tried to ram the doors down and he used ladders as well, but the Jews counterattacked and caused many losses among the Romans.

[84] *Book VI Chapter 2, page 298*

"But when Titus perceived that his endeavors to spare a foreign temple turned to the damage of his soldiers, and then be killed, he gave order to set the gates on fire."[85]

And now the soldiers had already put fire to the gates, and the silver that was over them quickly carried the flames to the wood that was within it, whence it spread itself all on the sudden, and caught hold on the cloisters.

Upon the Jews seeing this fire all about them, their spirits sunk together with their bodies, and they were under such astonishment, that not one of them made any haste, either to defend himself or to quench the fire, but they stood as mute spectators of it only. However, they did not so grieve at the loss of what was now burning, as to grow wiser thereby for the time to come; but as though the holy house itself had been on fire already, they whetted their passions against the Romans.

This fire prevailed during that day and the next also; for the soldiers were not able to burn all the cloisters that were round about together at one time, but only by pieces.

But then, on the next day, Titus commanded part of his army to quench the fire, and to make a road for the more easy marching up of the legions, while he himself gathered the commanders together."[86]

That is how they were able to enter with their horses and with great strength. The Jews were no longer able to resist it. Many died at the hands of this cavalry and those who fled found refuge in the innermost part of the Temple.

---

[85] *Book VI Chapter 4 page 306*

[86] *Book VI Chapter 4 page 307*

At that point, the valleys and ditches surrounding the wall were filled with rotting cadavers. Many who entered by horse, entered through the valleys and others arrived on foot to enter through the steps of the wall.

The blood reached the bits of the horses!

"So Titus retired into the tower of Antonia, and resolved to storm the temple the next day, early in the morning, with his whole army, and to encamp round about the holy house. But as for that house, God had, for certain, long ago doomed it to the fire; and now that fatal day was come, according to the revolution of ages; it was the tenth day[87] of the month Lous, [Ab,] upon which it was formerly burnt by the king of Babylon.

Although these flames took their rise from the Jews themselves, and were occasioned by them; for upon Titus's retiring, the seditious lay still for a little while, and then attacked the Romans again, when those that guarded the holy house fought with those that quenched the fire that was burning the inner [court of the] temple; but these Romans put the Jews to flight, and proceeded as far as the holy house itself."[88]

---

[87] *In some translations it states the 10th day and others state the 9th. For present day Israel, it is the 9th.*

[88] *Book VI Chapter 4 page 307*

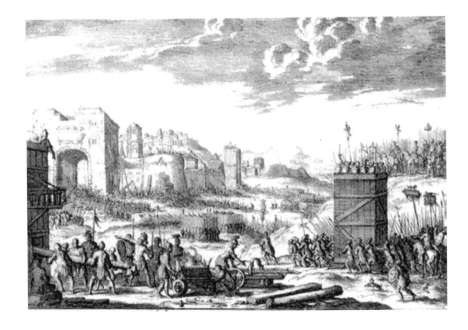

*Fig. 8 — The Siege and Destruction of Jerusalem
by Titus and Vespasian*

God Himself had accelerated the end because had such a
severe siege continued, they would have all died from
starvation and the wars would have extended throughout
Palestine and other places where the children of God found
refuge.

> *And unless those days were shortened, no flesh would
> be saved; but for the elect's sake those days will be
> shortened.*
>
> *Matthew 24:22*

Seeing the internal fortresses and towers the tyrants had abandoned, Titus declared: "Truly God was with us in this war, having removed the Jews from these strongholds because, "what could have machines or hands done to these towers?"

Fig. 9 — Jerusalem during Titus' final attack

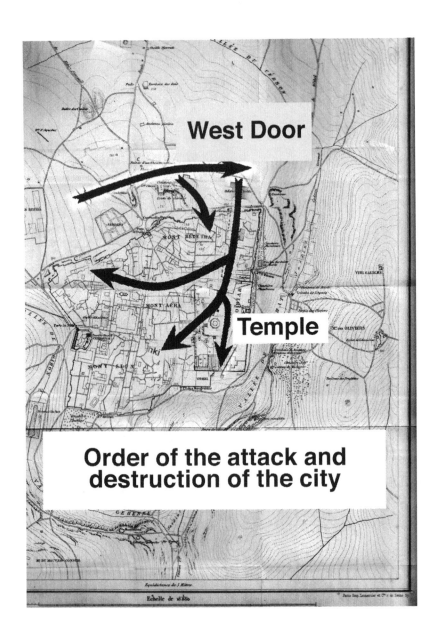

Fig. 10 — Order of the attack on Jerusalem

Fig. 11 — The walls are taken

3. How The Temple was burned against Titus' will

Josephus continues to narrate what took place:

"At which time one of the soldiers, without staying for any orders, and without any concern or dread upon him at so great an undertaking, and being hurried on by a certain divine fury, snatched somewhat out of the materials that were on fire, and being lifted up by another soldier, he set fire to a golden window, through which there was a passage to the rooms that were round about the holy house, on the north side of it.

As the flames went upward, the Jews made a great clamor, such as so mighty an affliction required, and ran together to prevent it; and now they spared not their lives any longer, nor suffered any thing to restrain their force, since that holy house was perishing, for whose sake it was that they kept such a guard about it."[89]

"And now a certain person came running to Titus, and told him of this fire, as he was resting himself in his tent after the last battle; whereupon he rose up in great haste, and, as he was, ran to the holy house, in order to have a stop put to the fire; after him followed all his commanders, and after them followed the several legions, in great astonishment."

"So there was a great clamor and tumult raised, as was natural upon the disorderly motion of so great an army. Then did Caesar, both by calling to the soldiers that were fighting, with a loud voice, and by giving a signal to them with his right hand, order them to quench the fire. But they did not hear what he said, though he spake so loud, having their ears already dimmed by a greater noise another way."

"But as for the legions that came running thither, neither any persuasions nor any threatenings could restrain their violence, but each one's own passion was his commander at this time."

"As they were crowding into the temple together, many of them were trampled on by one another, while a great number fell among the ruins of the cloisters, which were still hot and smoking, and were destroyed in the same miserable way with those whom they had conquered."

---

[89] *Book VI Chapter 4 page 308*

"When they were come near the holy house, they made as if they did not so much as hear Caesar's orders to the contrary; but they encouraged those that were before them to set it on fire. As for the seditious, they were in too great distress already to afford their assistance [towards quenching the fire]."

"They were every where slain, and every where beaten; and as for a great part of the people, they were weak and without arms, and had their throats cut wherever they were caught. Now round about the altar lay dead bodies heaped one upon another, as at the steps going up to it ran a great quantity of their blood, whither also the dead bodies that were slain above [on the altar] fell down."[90]

Fig. 12 — The Destruction of the Temple by Francesco Hayes

---

[90] *Book VI Chapter 4 page 308*

"And now, since Caesar was no way able to restrain the enthusiastic fury of the soldiers, and the fire proceeded on more and more, he went into the holy place of the temple, with his commanders, and saw it, with what was in it, which he found to be far superior to what the relations of foreigners contained, and not inferior to what we ourselves boasted of and believed about it."[91]

" But as the flame had not as yet reached to its inward parts, but was still consuming the rooms that were about the holy house, and Titus supposing what the fact was, that the house itself might yet he saved, he came in haste and endeavored to persuade the soldiers to quench the fire."

"Yet were their passions too hard for the regards they had for Caesar, and the dread they had of him who forbade them, as was their hatred of the Jews, and a certain vehement inclination to fight them, too hard for them also."

"Moreover, the hope of plunder induced many to go on, as having this opinion, that all the places within were full of money, and as seeing that all round about it was made of gold."

"And besides, one of those that went into the place prevented Caesar, when he ran so hastily out to restrain the soldiers, and threw the fire upon the hinges of the gate, in the dark; whereby the flame burst out from within the holy house itself immediately, when the commanders retired, and Caesar with them, and when nobody any longer forbade those that were without to set fire to it. And thus was the holy house burnt down, without Caesar's approbation."[92]

Fig. 13 — The Temple seized by the Roman Soldiers

"While the holy house was on fire, every thing was plundered that came to hand, and ten thousand of those that were caught were slain; nor was there a commiseration of any age, or any reverence of gravity, but children, and old men, and profane persons, and priests were all slain in the same manner; so that this war went round all sorts of men, and brought them to destruction, and as well those that made supplication for their lives, as those that defended themselves by fighting."

"The flame was also carried a long way, and made an echo, together with the groans of those that were slain; and because this hill was high, and the works at the temple were very great, one would have thought the whole city had been on fire."

---

[92] *Book VI Chapter 4 page 308*

"Nor can one imagine any thing either greater or more terrible than this noise; for there was at once a shout of the Roman legions, who were marching all together, and a sad clamor of the seditious, who were now surrounded with fire and sword. The people also that were left above were beaten back upon the enemy, and under a great consternation, and made sad moans at the calamity they were under; the multitude also that was in the city joined in this outcry with those that were upon the hill."

"Besides, many of those that were worn away by the famine, and their mouths almost closed, when they saw the fire of the holy house, they exerted their utmost strength, and brake out into groans and outcries again: Pera did also return the echo, as well as the mountains round about [the city,] and augmented the force of the entire noise."

"Yet was the misery itself more terrible than this disorder; for one would have thought that the hill itself, on which the temple stood, was seething hot, as full of fire on every part of it, that the blood was larger in quantity than the fire, and those that were slain more in number than those that slew them; for the ground did no where appear visible, for the dead bodies that lay on it; but the soldiers went over heaps of those bodies, as they ran upon such as fled from them."

"And now it was that the multitude of the robbers were thrust out [of the inner court of the temple by the Romans,] and had much ado to get into the outward court, and from thence into the city, while the remainder of the populace fled into the cloister of that outer court. As for the priests, some of them plucked up from the holy house the spikes that were upon it, with their bases, which were made of lead, and shot them at the Romans instead of darts."

"But then as they gained nothing by so doing, and as the fire burst out upon them, they retired to the wall that was eight cubits broad, and there they tarried; yet did two of these of eminence among them, who might have saved themselves by going over to the Romans, or have borne up with courage, and taken their fortune with the others, throw themselves into the fire, and were burnt together with the holy house; their names were Meirus the son of Belgas, and Joseph the son of Daleus."

"And now the Romans, judging that it was in vain to spare what was round about the holy house, burnt all those places, as also the remains of the cloisters and the gates, two excepted; the one on the east side, and the other on the south; both which, however, they burnt afterward. They also burnt down the treasury chambers, in which was an immense quantity of money, and an immense number of garments, and other precious goods there reposited; and, to speak all in a few words, there it was that the entire riches of the Jews were heaped up together, while the rich people had there built themselves chambers [to contain such furniture]."[93]

Jesus (the Lord) had given His people the opportunity to unite with His spirit and be free from that horrendous Judgment, but they did not receive it.

---

[93] *Book VI Chapter 5 page 310*

But they made light of it and went their ways, one to his own farm, another to his business.

And the rest seized his servants, treated them spitefully, and killed them. But when the king heard about it, he was furious.

And he sent out his armies, destroyed those murderers, and burned up their city.

Matthew 22:5-7

Rome tore Israel into Shreds

For wherever the carcass is, there the eagles will be gathered together.

Matthew 24:28

The image of this illustration is that of an enemy falling upon his victim. The eagles are the Roman legions and Jerusalem is the dead body, being devoured. Job says of the eagle:

Does the eagle mount up at your command, And make its nest on high?

On the rock it dwells and resides, On the crag of the rock and the stronghold.

From there it spies out the prey; Its eyes observe from afar.

Its young ones suck up blood; And where the slain are, there it is."

Job 39:27-30

False Prophets promise Salvation

For false christs and false prophets will rise and show great signs and wonders to deceive, if possible, even the elect.

Matthew 24:24

"The soldiers also came to the rest of the cloisters that were in the outer [court of the] temple, whither the women and children, and a great mixed multitude of the people, fled, in number about six thousand. But before Caesar had determined any thing about these people, or given the commanders any orders relating to them, the soldiers were in such a rage, that they set that cloister on fire; by which means it came to pass that some of these were destroyed by throwing themselves down headlong, and some were burnt in the cloisters themselves."

"Nor did any one of them escape with his life. A false prophet was the occasion of these people's destruction, who had made a public proclamation in the city that very day, that God commanded them to get upon the temple, and that there they should receive miraculous signs of their deliverance."

"Now there was then a great number of false prophets suborned by the tyrants to impose on the people, who denounced this to them, that they should wait for deliverance from God; and this was in order to keep them from deserting, and that they might be buoyed up above fear and care by such hopes."[94]

---

[94] *Book VI Chapter 5 Page 311*

"Because when a man is in the midst of adversity, he is easily persuaded by someone who wants to deceive him. They will believe just about anything, especially if they are told there is hope that they will be delivered from their bad situation. For sure the person in need believes because of the hope they need."[95]

That is how the Temple was burned down against Titus' will.

"Now although any one would justly lament the destruction of such a work as this was, since it was the most admirable of all the works that we have seen or heard of, both for its curious structure and its magnitude, and also for the vast wealth bestowed upon it, as well as for the glorious reputation it had for its holiness; yet might such a one comfort himself with this thought, that it was fate that decreed it so to be, which is inevitable, both as to living creatures, and as to works and places also."

"However, one cannot but wonder at the accuracy of this period thereto relating; for the same month and day were now observed, as I said before, wherein the holy house was burnt formerly by the Babylonians."

"Now the number of years that passed from its first foundation, which was laid by king Solomon, till this its destruction, which happened in the second year of the reign of Vespasian, are collected to be one thousand one hundred and thirty, besides seven months and fifteen days; and from

---

[95] *Book VI Chapter 5 section 2 (Different translation of the last paragraph)*

the second building of it, which was done by Haggai, in the second year of Cyrus the king, till its destruction under Vespasian, there were six hundred and thirty-nine years and forty-five days."[96]

For behold, the day is coming, Burning like an oven, And all the proud, yes, all who do wickedly will be stubble. And the day which is coming shall burn them up," Says the Lord of hosts, "That will leave them neither root nor branch. You shall trample the wicked, For they shall be ashes under the soles of your feet On the day that I do this," Says the Lord of hosts.

Malachi 4:1 & 3

Account of the Christians who had remained in Jerusalem

I found the following information regarding the Christians who remained in Jerusalem in the antique writings by Bishop Epiphanius.

"Bishop Epiphanius (310-403 A.D.), originally from Palestine wrote basing himself on documents from the II Century: "On his trip to the Orient, Emperor Adriano (138 A.D.) found that the temple of God had been destroyed and Jerusalem completely devastated with the exception of a few homes and the small church in Zion. The disciples had found shelter in its outer room on their way back from the Mount of Olives."

---

[96] *Book VI Chapter 4 page 309*

Fig. 14 — Destruction of Jerusalem by David Roberts (1850)

There were certain homes and seven synagogues that were built on Mount Zion that were safe from destruction. They were hidden like shacks.

The information given by Epiphanius is historically based on the fact that the neighborhood to the west of the city was outside of the camp of military operations during the conquering of Jerusalem in 70 A.D. and the attack began on the opposite side of the city.

It is very likely that this small church served as a place of shelter for some Christians that had not fled beforehand.

CHAPTER 11

THE SIGNS WHICH PRECEEDED AND WERE REVEALED BEFORE THE DESTRUCTION

And I will show wonders in the heavens and in the earth: Blood and fire and pillars of smoke. The sun shall be turned into darkness, and the moon into blood, before the coming of the great and awesome day of the Lord.

Joel 2:30-31

The sun had certainly darkened and the moon had turned red with the thick smoke caused by the burning of the city which was filled with blood and death.

But God had been longsuffering and abundant in mercy by sending signs and wonders before bringing His judgment, however thousands of Jews ignored them. They would laugh the same way they laughed at Noah when he announced the flood.

For as in the days before the flood, they were eating and drinking, marrying and giving in marriage, until the day that Noah entered the ark, and did not

know until the flood came and took them all away,
so also will the coming of the Son of Man be.

Matthew 24:38-39

The Comet in the shape of a Sword

"Thus were the miserable people persuaded by these deceivers, and such as believed God himself; while they did not attend nor give credit to the signs that were so evident, and did so plainly foretell their future desolation, but, like men infatuated, without either eyes to see or minds to consider, did not regard the denunciations that God made to them. Thus there was a star resembling a sword, which stood over the city, and a comet, that continued a whole year."[97]

Then the sign of the Son of Man will appear in
heaven, and then all the tribes of the earth will
mourn, and they will see the Son of Man coming on
the clouds of heaven with power and great glory.

Matthew 24:30

The signs took place one right after the other.

Light in The Altar

"Thus also before the Jews' rebellion, and before those commotions which preceded the war, when the people were

---

[97] *Book VI Chapter 5 page 311*

come in great crowds to the feast of unleavened bread, on the eighth day of the month Xanthicus, [Nisan,] and at the ninth hour of the night, so great a light shone round the altar and the holy house, that it appeared to be bright day time; which lasted for half an hour. This light seemed to be a good sign to the unskillful, but was so interpreted by the sacred scribes, as to portend those events that followed immediately upon it."[98]

The Ox that gave birth to a Lamb and the door made of copper that opened

At the same festival also, a heifer, as she was led by the high priest to be sacrificed, brought forth a lamb in the midst of the temple. Moreover, the eastern gate of the inner [court of the] temple, which was of brass, and vastly heavy, and had been with difficulty shut by twenty men, and rested upon a basis armed with iron, and had bolts fastened very deep into the firm floor, which was there made of one entire stone, was seen to be opened of its own accord about the sixth hour of the night. Now those that kept watch in the temple came hereupon running to the captain of the temple, and told him of it; who then came up thither, and not without great difficulty was able to shut the gate again. This also appeared to the vulgar to be a very happy prodigy, as if God did thereby open them the gate of happiness. But the men of learning understood it, that the security of their holy house was dissolved of its own accord, and that the gate was opened for the advantage of their enemies. So these publicly declared that the signal foreshowed the desolation that was coming upon them.[99]

---

[98] *Book VI Chapter 5 page 311*

[99] *Book VI Chapter 5 page 311*

The Sign of The Son of Man, The Chariots in Heaven

Jesus told the High Priest when He was interrogated about whether He was the Christ:

> *Jesus said to him, "It is as you said. Nevertheless, I say to you, hereafter you will see the Son of Man sitting at the right hand of the Power, and coming on the clouds of heaven."*
>
> *Matthew 26:64*

> *When the Son of Man comes in His glory, and all the holy angels with Him, then He will sit on the throne of His glory. 32 All the nations will be gathered before Him, and He will separate them one from another, as a shepherd divides his sheep from the goats.*
>
> *Matthew 25:31-32*

Josephus was a witness to this:

"Besides these, a few days after that feast, on the one and twentieth day of the month Artemisius, [Jyar,] a certain prodigious and incredible phenomenon appeared: I suppose the account of it would seem to be a fable, were it not related by those that saw it, and were not the events that followed it of so considerable a nature as to deserve such signals; for, before sun-setting, chariots and troops of soldiers in their armor were seen running about among the clouds, and surrounding of cities. Moreover, at that feast which we call Pentecost, as the priests were going by night into the inner [court of the temple,] as their custom was, to perform their sacred ministrations, they said that, in the first place, they felt a quaking, and heard a great noise, and after that they heard a sound as of a great multitude, saying, "Let us remove hence."[100]

When I read this, I could not help but think that the person who wrote this was Jewish and not converted. Christian writings do not exist about this period of tribulation or they have not yet been discovered. There is complete silence on behalf of Christians regarding where else we can extract information from. I ask myself: Did they hear this also from the mountains, caves or other places of refuge? Did the alleged refugees on Mount Zion hear it or was it only heard upon Jerusalem? Because this took place during Pentecost it means that these signs occurred two months before the complete destruction of the city.

The Voice of The Prophet and The Groaning

"But, what is still more terrible, there was one Jesus, the son of Ananus, a plebeian and a husbandman, who, four years before the war began, and at a time when the city was in very great peace and prosperity, came to that feast whereon it is our custom for every one to make tabernacles to God in the temple, began on a sudden to cry aloud, "A voice from the east, a voice from the west, a voice from the four winds, a voice against Jerusalem and the holy house, a voice against the bridegrooms and the brides, and a voice against this whole people!" This was his cry, as he went about by day and by night, in all the lanes of the city."

[100] *Book VI Chapter 5 page 311*

It will be as in the days of Noah. They will marry and give themselves in marriage, but they will not listen just like they did not listen to Noah at the time. [101]

"However, certain of the most eminent among the populace had great indignation at this dire cry of his, and took up the man, and gave him a great number of severe stripes; yet did not he either say any thing for himself, or any thing peculiar to those that chastised him, but still went on with the same words which he cried before. Hereupon our rulers, supposing, as the case proved to be, that this was a sort of divine fury in the man, brought him to the Roman procurator, where he was whipped till his bones were laid bare; yet he did not make any supplication for himself, nor shed any tears, but turning his voice to the most lamentable tone possible, at every stroke of the whip his answer was, "Woe, woe to Jerusalem!"

Therefore, indeed, I send you prophets, wise men, and scribes: some of them you will kill and crucify, and some of them you will scourge in your synagogues and persecute from city to city, that on you may come all the righteous blood shed on the earth, from the blood of righteous Abel to the blood of Zechariah, son of Berechiah, whom you murdered between the temple and the altar. Assuredly, I say to you, all these things will come upon this generation.

"*O Jerusalem, Jerusalem, the one who kills the prophets and stones those who are sent to her! How often I wanted to gather your children together, as a hen gathers her chicks under her wings, but you were*

---

[101] *Paraphrases of Matthew 24:38 and 39*

*not willing! See! Your house is left to you desolate; for
I say to you, you shall see Me no more till you say,
'Blessed is He who comes in the name of the Lord!' "*

Matthew 23:34-38

"And when Albinus (for he was then our procurator) asked him, Who he was? and whence he came? and why he uttered such words? he made no manner of reply to what he said, but still did not leave off his melancholy ditty, till Albinus took him to be a madman, and dismissed him."

"Now, during all the time that passed before the war began, this man did not go near any of the citizens, nor was seen by them while he said so; but he every day uttered these lamentable words, as if it were his premeditated vow, "Woe, woe to Jerusalem!""

"Nor did he give ill words to any of those that beat him every day, nor good words to those that gave him food; but this was his reply to all men, and indeed no other than a melancholy presage of what was to come. This cry of his was the loudest at the festivals; and he continued this ditty for seven years and five months, without growing hoarse, or being tired therewith, until the very time that he saw his presage in earnest fulfilled in our siege, when it ceased; for as he was going round upon the wall, he cried out with his utmost force, "Woe, woe to the city again, and to the people, and to the holy house!""

"And just as he added at the last, "Woe, woe to myself also!" there came a stone out of one of the engines, and smote him, and killed him immediately; and as he was uttering the very same passages he gave up the ghost."

"Now if any one consider these things, he will find that God takes care of mankind, and by all ways possible foreshows to our race what is for their preservation; but that men perish by those miseries which they madly and voluntarily bring upon themselves; for the Jews, by demolishing the tower of Antonia, had made their temple four-square, while at the same time they had it written in their sacred oracles, "That then should their city be taken, as well as their holy house, when once their temple should become four-square."

" But now, what did the most elevate them in undertaking this war, was an ambiguous oracle that was also found in their sacred writings, how," about that time, one from their country should become governor of the habitable earth." The Jews took this prediction to belong to themselves in particular, and many of the wise men were thereby deceived in their determination. Now this oracle certainly denoted the government of Vespasian, who was appointed emperor as he was in Judea."

"However, it is not possible for men to avoid fate, although they see it beforehand. But these men interpreted some of these signals according to their own pleasure, and some of them they utterly despised, until their madness was demonstrated, both by the taking of their city and their own destruction."[102]

---

[102] *Book VI Chapter 5 pages 311 and 312*

CHAPTER 12

THE FINAL STAGE

Following the destruction of the Temple, the city was burned as well. According to Josephus over one million one hundred thousand Jews were killed.

The Jews who did survive were taken prisoner to the city of Caesarea by the sea, where Titus would amuse himself by having big parties and spectacles. He would throw the Jews to the beasts or would have them fight among each other in the arena as if they were true enemies.

Simon, who hid among his people in the sewers of the city, one day decided to come out and deceive everyone pretending to be the ghost of the Messiah.

He dressed in a white tunic with a golden belt and placed a red robe upon his shoulders. He then came out from the sewers and walked among the Temple ruins. Everyone who saw him was shocked and speechless, but the captain of Titus' army, Terrence Rufus discovered who he was and took him prisoner before Titus, who had prepared a very cruel end to his life.

His exit from the sewer tunnels caused the discovery of his followers and they were arrested as well.

Titus then organized a big party to celebrate his brother's birthday and killed a large part of the prisoners in his honor. There were 2,500 men thrown to the beasts, set on fire while others died fighting among each other in the scuffle. To the Romans, this still seemed as too small of a punishment for the Jews and felt they deserved even more.

Simon Bar Giora and John of Giscala were among the prisoners in the annual triumphant parade celebrated in Rome the following year. The first of the two tyrants was executed later and the second was imprisoned for life.

The last of the Zealots, thieves and the wicked men who survived, fled to the fortress of Masada. This is where they committed mass suicide three and a half years later because they refused to give themselves up during the Roman invasion. This is the detailed account how Israel was completely destroyed.

CONCLUSION

Understanding what took place in history leads us to re-evaluate many things that we have given a futuristic application to.

The search for truth is accomplished in only one way and that is asking The Holy Spirit.

> *But the Helper, the Holy Spirit, whom the Father will send in My name, He will teach you all things, and bring to your remembrance all things that I said to you.*
>
> *John 14:26*

Men can debate in a thousand ways. Some believe one thing while others reason something else. Following the opinion of man leads to the danger of erring.
God left us the Spirit to inquire of Him all truth. Who, but Him, has the correct interpretation of all things?

As a Prophet and having a Doctorate in Theology, I can only place before you what I have received.

What I have seen and heard has led me to a powerful life of revelation and communion with The Father, The Son and The Holy Spirit. I live the power and the authority of The Kingdom that He left us and it is an extraordinary walk.

"...the Spirit of truth, whom the world cannot receive, because it neither sees Him nor knows Him; but you know Him, for He dwells with you and will be in you. I will not leave you orphans; I will come to you.

A little while longer and the world will see Me no more, but you will see Me. Because I live, you will live also."

John 14:17-19

This is what I truly and genuinely live and believe. This is my legacy for whoever wants to receive it.

The Kingdom of God is among us and we no longer have to wait for anything. We must take it and enjoy it in the full measure that He gives.

QUESTIONS THAT ARISE WHILE READING THIS BOOK

1.) What is The Marriage Supper of The Lamb?

Marriage in the natural is consummated when man and woman become one flesh in intimacy; when she becomes flesh of his flesh and bone of his bone. Paul the Apostle clearly writes about this:

> *For the husband is head of the wife, as also Christ is head of the church; and He is the Savior of the body.*

> *For no one ever hated his own flesh, but nourishes and cherishes it, just as the Lord does the church. For we are members of His body, of His flesh and of His bones. "For this reason a man shall leave his father and mother and be joined to his wife, and the two shall become one flesh." This is a great mystery, but I speak concerning Christ and the church.*

> *Ephesians 5:23 & 29-32*

> *But he who is joined to the Lord is one spirit with Him.*

> *1 Corinthians 6:17*

It is made very clear in these scriptures that in order to be the body of Christ, we must be joined to Him as His wife.

When a man and a woman get married, they become one flesh. In the same way, when we marry Jesus, we become ONE SPIRIT with Him. When He said, *"It is finished"* He meant that the work was completed.

Through His blood, He washed us completely and absolutely. In His blood, there are no longer blemishes or wrinkles; we are white as snow. This is the work of grace.

Understanding this makes all the difference. If we are simply the bride of Christ or His fiancé, hoping to marry Him in the future, we are not yet His flesh. The bride does not have legal access to anything that belongs to the man, but once she marries him, she has access to everything. The check book of the King is only accessible to the wife. The bride cannot have intimacy with her beloved until they are married.

An "engaged or betrothed" woman in the Jewish tradition was considered the husband's possession, but she could not have intimacy with him until the wedding day nor could she live with him. They were not able to dwell together until after the wedding.

Jesus said:

I do not pray for these alone, but also for those who will believe in Me through their word; that they all may be one, as You, Father, are in Me, and I in You; that they also may be one in Us, that the world may believe that You sent Me.

John 17:20-21

In order for the Father and the Son to be "ONE IN Us" there has to be a marriage union.

This is a very important subject, because as long as we are waiting for The marriage of the Lamb, in an unknown future, we will not have access to anything; and that is where the devil robs our power, our riches and the entrance into The King's chambers, as well as the Glory of the first coming of the Messiah.

Apostle John Eckhart wrote in his book, *"Behold I Come Quickly"*:

"This eschatological wedding is the fulfillment of the promise given by God to Israel, which was engaged to be married to **Him.** (Hosea 2:19-20). This marriage engagement was through Jesus and the New Covenant with the Church of the first century, composed of Jews and Gentiles. The invitation to the wedding was given in the first century. At the time, everything was already prepared for it to take place. Many have tried to place this wedding at the end of the Christian Age instead of the Jewish Age."

"The parable of the Ten Virgins (Matthew 25) reflects this engagement between Christ and His Church. The Lord went to prepare a place for His Church and would return to take her to the marriage bed. The five prudent virgins were prepared for His return, but the five foolish virgins were not ready. The oil represents the anointing and living through the Holy Spirit. Jesus spoke to this generation."

"The marriage supper of the Lamb would take place soon (Revelation 1:1, 3 and 19:7-9). John the Baptist rejoiced when he heard the voice of the bridegroom (John 3:19). All of this has an application for the first century. Jesus, the bridegroom had come to the world and was calling His Church to the wedding. The engagement was prophesied by Hosea (Hosea 2:19-20). "The parable of the ten virgins reflects the Jewish customs in the days of Jesus. The bridegroom was delayed because He was preparing a place for His bride in His Father's house. Once the place was prepared, the bridegroom would return for her."

"(John 14:1-3). At that point, the bride and groom go to the Father's house to celebrate the wedding and the feasts."

And I heard, as it were, the voice of a great multitude, as the sound of many waters and as the sound of mighty thunderings, saying, "Alleluia! For the Lord God Omnipotent reigns! Let us be glad and rejoice and give Him glory, for the marriage of the Lamb has come, and His wife has made herself ready.

Revelation 19:6-7

"The Kingdom of God was manifested through the judgments of Babylon, (Apostate Israel). The saints rejoice with the arrival of the wedding since they could now receive the blessings of the kingdom which had been finished."

This is what the Apostles taught as far as what the primitive Church should wait for and receive."

"Jesus prepared the dwelling to join together with us as the husband prepares a home for his wife.

> *In My Father's house are many mansions; if it were not so, I would have told you. I go to prepare a place for you. And if I go and prepare a place for you, I will come again and receive you to Myself; that where I am, there you may be also.*
>
> *John 14:2-3*[103]

Those who are not the wife are not the Tabernacle of God in the Earth.

2.) How Was The *Second Coming* Prophesied in The Old Testament?

The Old Testament recognizes only one physical coming of The Messiah which is intimately related with the establishment of The Kingdom of God.

---

[103] *John Eckhart "Behold I Come Quickly" Pages 161-162*

For unto us a Child is born, unto us a Son is given; and the government will be upon His shoulder. And His name will be called Wonderful, Counselor, Mighty God, Everlasting Father, Prince of Peace. Of the increase of His government and peace there will be no end, upon the throne of David and over His kingdom, to order it and establish it with judgment and justice from that time forward, even forever. The zeal of the Lord of hosts will perform this.

Isaiah 9:6-7

The Throne of David is not the throne of a mortal man, but the throne of the Messiah. Jesus said that His kingdom was **not of this world**, therefore neither is His Throne.

Not once do we see throughout the Old Testament or in the words of Jesus a "Churchage" and thousands of years later, "The Kingdom Age" as dispensationalists claim.

His presence in the clouds to receive the Kingdom and give it to His saints is also prophesied. Jesus sat on the Throne with His Father and His Kingdom has no end.

I was watching in the night visions, and behold, one like the Son of Man, coming with the clouds of heaven! He came to the Ancient of Days, and they brought Him near before Him. Then to Him was given dominion and glory and a kingdom, that all peoples, nations, and languages should serve Him. His dominion is an everlasting dominion, which shall not pass away, and His kingdom the one which shall not be destroyed.

Daniel 7:13-14

In the same way, a manifestation of Judgment would come as we have seen throughout this book.

3.) At what Point in Time Does The Lord Come and Split The Mount of Olives in Two?

The Mount of Olives is a symbol of Israel. Mountains are a symbol of authority, and in this case, represent Israel's priesthood. This passage is linked to the judgment of 70 A.D. when Israel was scattered and its Priestly authority came to an end.

One part of Israel followed the Messiah and was saved. The other was destroyed or scattered.

And in that day His feet will stand on the Mount of Olives, which faces Jerusalem on the east. And the Mount of Olives shall be split in two, from east to west, making a very large valley; Half of the mountain shall move toward the north and half of it toward the south. Then you shall flee through My mountain valley, for the mountain valley shall reach to Azal. Yes, you shall flee as you fled from the earthquake in the days of Uzziah king of Judah.

Zachariah 14:4-5

4.) If Jesus came in the clouds at the Judgment of 70 A.D., how should we wait for Him now?

We should remember that He came to bring a Spiritual Kingdom and He adheres to His design.

The manifestation of Jesus takes many forms.

He spoke not only of His coming during the judgment, but also spoke of *a spiritual coming* in which He and His Father would make their dwelling in us.

This is a reality which the body of Christ must grow into and experience as the most powerful reality within our spirit. *We are His body, the fullness of Him who fills all in all! (Ephesians 1:23)*

He is the vine and we are the branches. The believer is powerfully joined to Him if this is his reality.

In the New Testament various words are used to describe Jesus in His coming or in the way He comes or is manifested.

The scriptures which mention His coming are described with different words: *Parousia, Epiphania, Apocalipsis, Erchomai, Diafanes* and *Optanomai.* They all have to do with a revelation which makes Him present in different ways:

In the midst of His Church, within the believer and in the midst of the congregation, which is His Temple, in judgments on the Earth, in manifestations of glory that bring awakenings and revivals.

The fact that there are several words used to describe His coming and that are so different, leads us to believe that they are not just referring to *one coming*, but there are *many ways* in which He manifests.

Let us analyze these words:

HIS VISIBLE MANIFESTATIONS

Erchomai:[104] To come in time. "aoristo"

"The aoristo refers to a length of duration of time that is of no interest to the one speaking. It is often such an insignificant amount of time that it is reduced to a point (punctual). The Greek term aorist signified **'undefined, unlimited, with no time limit.'** It was originally something like "no time;" a verb with no direct translation such as eternity or **"forever and ever."**[105]

---

[104] *Strongs Concordance 2064. Ercomai; middle voice of a primary verb (used only in the present and imperfect tense, the others being supplied by a kindred (middle voice)*

[105] *Hispanoteca, language and culture, forum-Justo Fernando Lopez.*

The aorist denotes an action that is occurring in the past and not making reference to its progress or expressing that the action has been completed.

The aorist simply presents the action and does not make reference to the duration. The aoristo does not express duration or term; it is undetermined or undefined.

The aoristo is definitely not a particular time or the future. In this particular verse, Jesus was prophesying that He would come to stay spiritually and eternally in the midst of His people.

> *"I am the Alpha and the Omega, the Beginning and the End," says the Lord, "who is and who was and who is to come (erchomai), the Almighty."*

> *Revelation 1:8*

We also find this same word in Acts 1:11 and John 14:18 among others.

Parousia:[106] We also saw "Presence" in Chapter 1.

> *For we did not follow cunningly devised fables when we made known to you the power and coming of our Lord Jesus Christ, but were eyewitnesses of His majesty.*

> *2 Peter 1:16*

---

[106] *3952 parousía (from parōn, "be present, arrive to enter into a situation") Of the present participle of 3918; a close being, that is to say, arrival (often, return, specifically of Christ to punish Jerusalem, or finally, the evil ones), (by implication) physical, aspect: Will come, the presence. Strongs Biblical Concordance*

We also find it in other verses such as 1 John 2:28 and 2 Peter 3:12.

Apocalipsis:[107] *(apokalupsis)* Revelation

Apocalipsis (Apokalupsis). This word means revelation, illumination, and apparition. It is when the Father or Jesus reveals something concerning Himself to man's heart. In the Book of Revelation or *"Apocalipse"*, which is the revelation of Jesus Christ, we are submerged in His prophetic realm to see and understand His heavenly character and how He acts. It is when He brings out His hidden treasures and brings them to light. It is also the revelation of the sentences of all judgments.

The Father reveals that Jesus is The Christ/The Messiah to Peter.

> *Jesus answered and said to him, "Blessed are you, Simon Bar-Jonah, for flesh and blood has not revealed (Apocalypse) this to you, but My Father who is in heaven.*
>
> *Matthew 16:17*
>
> *so that you come short in no gift, eagerly waiting for the revelation (Apocalypse) of our Lord Jesus Christ*
>
> *1 Corinthians 1:7*

---

[107] *602. From 601; revelation: - appears, comes, hurry, the manifestation, be revealed, revelation Strongs Biblical Concordance.*

MANIFESTATIONS OF LIGHT

Epiphainooe:[108] It is the splendor of His Presence. We see it manifested in God's judgments or when He wants to bring new revelation and understanding to His Church. It is not necessarily visible to our eyes, but to our spirit. It is the Epiphainooe of Jesus, which shines in our hearts for the illumination of the knowledge of the Glory of God. (2 Corinthians 4:6)

I charge you therefore before God and the Lord Jesus Christ, who will judge the living and the dead at[a] His appearing Epiphainooe and His kingdom:

2 Timothy 4:1

Diaphanes: Splendor, Clarity-this word, just like the previous one is the splendor of His light in us. We see this word in 2 Timothy.

Finally, there is laid up for me the crown of righteousness, which the Lord, the righteous Judge, will give to me on that Day, and not to me only but also to all who have loved His appearing Diaphanes.

2 Timothy 4:8

We will also find it 2 Thessalonians 2:8

---

[108] *Strong's Concordance 2014. epiphainooe; from 1909 and 5316; to shine upon, i.e. become (literally) visible or (figuratively) known: appear - give light.*

Optanomai:[109] To see something magnificent (not related to a grammatical subject)

> *to whom He also presented Himself alive after His suffering by many infallible proofs, being seen (optanomai) by them during forty days and speaking of the things pertaining to the kingdom of God.*

> *Acts 1:8*

5.) Does any part of Scripture state that He will come back in the Flesh?

First of all, we must understand that He is no longer made of flesh and bone like us, but His body was glorified.

After His resurrection, in that condition He walked through walls and appeared in the midst of His disciples. He had a different appearance since not even Mary recognized Him outside of the tomb and neither did His disciples.

He told Mary not to touch Him since He still needed to go to the Father and then He would return immediately. That is what He did and afterwards He appeared to His disciples.. Thomas placed his hand on His side. He did touch Him because He had already gone to His Father.

---

[109] *Optomai: I appear, am seen, let myself be seen Strongs Concordance 4648 a watching from a distance): Appear — look, see, shew self.*

After His resurrection He never slept with His disciples again or remained on the Earth. He appeared to them everyday during forty days and went back and forth to Heaven. He did not need to remain here. He rules from Heaven.

If it were so, He would have told us to wait for His earthly kingdom in Jerusalem. He never said such a thing. He specifically said that His Kingdom was not of this world.

6.) Why was Israel re-established in 1948?

God promised Israel that their territory would belong to them forever. He gave it back to them out of love.

This does not mean, as some believe, that God is in covenant with Israel to establish the Temple once again and return to the old system of sacrifices.

God already made the perfect sacrifice by sending His Son as the Passover Lamb that put an end to the old system.

Jesus declared in His Glory that He made all things new.

Anyone can drink from Him, Jew or Greek. There are no more nationalities in Him. He is the King over all the earth and His Priesthood is according to Melchizedek, not according to Aaron.

Then He who sat on the throne said, "Behold, I make all things new." And He said to me, "Write, for these words are true and faithful."

Revelation 21:5

God did not give the Jews back their land to kill them once again and to destroy Jerusalem. This already occurred.

His Kingdom is upon Jerusalem and upon the rest of the earth.

God destroyed the old Jerusalem so we would no longer place our eyes on earthly things, but instead on heavenly things instead.

He made a New Jerusalem, in order not to build the old one.

This is our new citizenship and His Tabernacle is in the midst of men.

God Reigns! Let the Earth Rejoice!

7.) Why Does Scripture say that all of Israel shall be saved?

And so all Israel will be saved, as it is written: "The Deliverer will come out of Zion, and He will turn away ungodliness from Jacob;

Romans 11:26

This scripture refers to the true Israel that was saved in the midst of the judgment in 70 A.D.

Jesus warned John in Revelation to be weary of satan's synagogue and those who claimed to be Jewish and were not, but lied.

Indeed I will make those of the synagogue of satan, who say they are Jews and are not, but lie—indeed I will make them come and worship before your feet, and to know that I have loved you.

Revelation 3:9

Paul also writes that not all Jews are true Jews, but those who are Jews, are by faith:

For he is not a Jew who is one outwardly, nor is circumcision that which is outward in the flesh; but he is a Jew who is one inwardly; and circumcision is that of the heart, in the Spirit, not in the letter; whose praise is not from men but from God.

Romans 2:28-29

Paul also says that only a remnant will be saved.

Isaiah also cries out concerning Israel:

"Though the number of the children of Israel be as the sand of the sea, the remnant will be saved. For He will finish the work and cut it short in righteousness, because the Lord will make a short work upon the earth."

Romans 9:27-28

Abraham's sons are the Jews by faith. *The Father waited to give everyone an opportunity to respond to the salvation from His Son, the Messiah.* All of these who did, the true Israel was saved.

I answer many other questions related to the Book of Revelation and The Kingdom among us in my book, *"Apocalypse: The Revelation of Jesus Christ."*

THE END

Participate in our

On Demand Courses

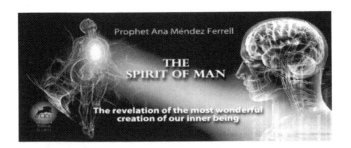

at.votlm.com

Mary,
The Mother of Jesus

By: Dr. Ana Méndez Ferrell

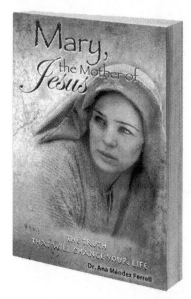

Discover who Mary really was and her message versus
the counterfeit Mary that has deceived millions.
A real eye-opener!

www.voiceofthelight.com

Voice Of The Light Ministries

www.voiceofthelight.com

904-834-2447

P.O. Box 3418

Ponte Vedra, FL 32004

USA

Made in the USA
Charleston, SC
21 August 2016